QUICK RESUME GUIDE

Six Steps to Building an Effective Resume

Michael Farr

and

The Editors @ JIST

Contents

JIST Works
America's Career Publisher

Quick Resume Guide

© 2010 by JIST Publishing

Published by JIST Works, an imprint of JIST Publishing
875 Montreal Way
St. Paul, MN 55102
E-mail: info@jist.com

> Visit our Web site at **www.jist.com** for information on JIST, tables of contents, sample pages, and ordering instructions for our many products! Please contact our Sales Department at www.jist.com for a free catalog and more information.

Workbook Product Manager: Lori Cates Hand
Cover and Interior Designer: Aleata Halbig
Page Layout: Toi Davis
Proofreader: Jeanne Clark

Printed in the United States of America
17 16 15 14 13 12   11 10 9 8 7 6 5

We have been careful to provide accurate information in this book, but it is possible that errors and omissions have been introduced. Please consider this in making any career plans or other important decisions. Trust your own judgment above all else and in all things.

ISBN 978-1-59357-790-2

The Six Steps for Writing an Effective Resume Fast

Even though a resume alone won't get you a job, it's hard to get an interview—much less a job—without one. And the faster you can write a resume and get it into circulation, the sooner you will be able to get out there and network, interview, and get a job.

Once you get your resume out there, you can take time later to improve it. It also helps to have other job seeking tools ready, such as cover letters, JIST Cards, and thank-you notes. This book shows you how to create all the documents you'll need to look for a job by following six steps:

1. Learn Resume Basics

2. Write a Simple Resume in About an Hour

3. Create a Skills Resume in Just a Few Hours

4. Develop a Cover Letter and Other Job Search Correspondence

5. Use Your Resume on the Internet

6. Improve and Perfect Your Resume

So without further delay, let's get started!

STEP 1: Learn Resume Basics

This book's ultimate objective is to help you get a good job in less time. Creating a superior resume alone will not get you a job. No matter how good your resume is, you will still have to get interviews and do well in them before you get a job offer.

So, a legitimate question might be "Why have a resume at all?" This chapter answers that question and then gives you an overview of some guidelines for writing your resume and tips on how to use it.

What Is a Resume and Why Do You Need One?

A resume is a one- or two-page summary of your life and employment history. Although resumes traditionally have been submitted on paper, they are increasingly sent in electronic form over the Internet. Whatever a resume's form, the idea is to select specific parts of your past that demonstrate that you can do a particular job well.

A resume presents you to prospective employers who—based on their response to the resume—may or may not grant you an interview. Along with the application, the resume is the tool employers use most often to screen job seekers.

For a variety of reasons, many career professionals suggest that resumes aren't needed at all. Some of these reasons make a lot of sense.

- **Resumes aren't good job search tools.** Trying to get an interview by submitting lots of unsolicited resumes is usually a waste of effort. There are better ways to get in to see people, such as networking with people you know and just picking up the phone to talk to those you don't.

- **Some jobs don't require resumes.** Particularly for entry-level, trade, or unskilled positions, resumes typically aren't required.

- **Some job search methods don't require resumes.** Many people get jobs without using a resume at all. These people get interviews because the employer knows them or they are referred by someone.

But there are several good reasons to have a resume:

- **Employers often ask for resumes.** If an employer asks for a resume (and many do), why make excuses? This alone is reason enough to have one.

- **Resumes help structure your communications.** A good resume requires you to clarify your job objective; select related skills, education, work, or other experiences; and list accomplishments—and present all this in a concise format. Doing these things is an essential step in your job search.

- **A properly used resume can be an effective job search tool.** A well-done resume presents details of your experiences efficiently so that an employer can refer to them as needed. It can also be used as a tool to present the skills you have to support your job objective and to reveal details that are often not solicited in a preliminary interview.

Types of Resumes

The three most common and useful resume types are the following:

- **Chronological:** Contains a listing of the jobs you've held, in reverse-chronological order. It highlights previous job titles, locations, dates employed, accomplishments, and tasks. Most employers prefer this format; however, it's often not good for people who have limited work experience, want to do something different, or have job gaps.

- **Skills or functional:** Instead of listing your experience under each job, this resume style clusters your experiences under major skill areas. For example, if you are strong in "communication skills," you could list a variety of work and other experiences under that heading. Although a skills resume is often more difficult to write than a chronological resume, it might be a better way to present your strengths if you have limited paid work experience, are changing careers, or have not worked for a while.

- **Combination:** You can combine elements of both the chronological and skills formats in various ways to improve the clarity or presentation of a resume. This is often a good compromise when your experience is limited but an employer still wants to see a chronological listing of your work history. You can begin the resume with a skills format but still include a section that lists your jobs in order, along with the dates you held them.

Step 2 helps you write a chronological resume. Step 3 shows you how to write a skills resume.

Attorneys, college professors, physicians, scientists, and various other occupations have their own rules or guidelines for preparing a "Curriculum Vitae" (CV) or some other special format. These specialized and occupation-specific resumes are not within the scope of this book and examples are not included, but many books provide information on them.

Just the Facts About Writing and Using Resumes

Many of these guidelines assume a traditional, printed-on-paper format rather than a resume that is submitted electronically (more on that in step 5). But you will likely need a paper resume *and* an electronic resume, and this advice will help in either case.

- **Length:** Opinions differ on length, but one to two pages is usually enough. If you are a recent high school or college graduate, keep your resume to one page. If you can't get everything on one page, you are better off filling up two full pages with content or more white space than providing one-and-a-half pages of content. If you are seeking a managerial, professional, or technical position—where most people have lots of prior experience—two pages is the norm.

- **Accuracy:** The majority of employers say they will throw away a resume if it has a typo on it. Even if you are good at proofreading, find someone else to review your resume, too—carefully. If possible, wait at least one day after you've written it before reading your draft. That delay will allow you to notice what your resume says, rather than what you think it says. Then, after you've read your resume, read it again to make sure you catch the errors. Then go over it again.

> *Even if you spell-check your resume on your computer, you still won't catch all the errors. For example, spell-check won't tell you that you should use "their" instead of "they're" in cases that call for a possessive pronoun. So there is no substitute for proofing your resume carefully.*

- **Appearance:** Your resume's overall appearance will affect an employer's opinion of you. In a matter of seconds, the employer will form a positive or negative opinion. Is your resume well laid out? Is it crisp and professional looking? Does it include good use of white space? Was it printed with a high-quality printer on good white or ivory paper? Does the envelope match the paper?

- **Accomplishments:** Don't simply list what your duties were; emphasize what you got done! Make sure you mention specific skills you have to do the job, as well as any accomplishments and credentials. Even a simple resume can include some of these elements.

- **Conciseness:** Write a long rough draft and then edit, edit, edit. If a word or phrase does not support your job objective, consider dropping it.

- **Authenticity:** It is most important that your resume represent you. Although you can use ideas and even words or phrases you like from the sample resumes in this book, you must present your own skills and support them with your own accomplishments. Make sure your resume ends up sounding like you wrote it.

This will be *your* resume, so you can do whatever makes sense to you. There are few resume rules that can't be broken if you have a good reason.

In the rest of this and the next two steps, you will learn about the types of resumes and see a few basic examples. Remember that it is often far more useful to you to have an acceptable resume as soon as possible—and use it in an active job search—than to delay your job search while working on a better resume. A better resume can come later, after you have created a presentable one that you can use right away.

4

Quick Resume Guide © JIST Works. Duplication Prohibited.

Seven Steps to Getting a Job Fast

In an active job search, you network and call potential employers for interviews. You don't wait for employers to respond to your resume. Here are the key elements of getting a good job in less time:

1. **Know your skills.** If you don't know what you are good at, how can you expect anyone else to figure it out? One employer survey found that about 80 percent of those who made it to the interview did not do a good job presenting the skills they had to do the job. If you don't know what you are good at and how this relates to a particular job, you can't write a good resume, can't do a good interview, and are unlikely to get a good job.

2. **Have a clear job objective.** If you don't know where you want to go, it will be difficult to get there. You can write a resume without having a job objective in mind, but it won't be a good one.

3. **Know where and how to look.** Because three out of four jobs are not advertised, you will have to use nontraditional job search techniques to find them.

4. **Spend at least 25 hours a week looking.** Most job seekers spend far less than this and, as a result, are unemployed longer than they need to be. So, if you want to get a better job in less time, plan on spending more time on your job search.

5. **Organize your time to get two interviews a day.** It sounds impossible but this can be done once you redefine what counts as an interview: An interview is any face-to-face contact with someone who can hire or supervise a person with your skills—even if no opening exists at the time.

6. **Do well in interviews.** You are unlikely to get a job offer unless you do well in this critical situation. You can improve your interview performance relatively easily. Knowing what skills you have and being able to support them with examples is a good start.

7. **Follow up on all job leads.** Following up can make a big difference in the results you get in your search for a new job.

STEP 2: Write a Simple Resume in About an Hour

You *can* write a basic resume in about an hour. It will not be a fancy one, and you might want to write a better one later, but I suggest you do the simple one first. Even if you decide to create a more sophisticated resume later (see step 6), doing one now will allow you to use it in your job search within 24 hours.

A chronological resume is easy to do. It works best for people who have had several years of experience in the same type of job they are seeking now. This is because a chronological resume clearly displays your recent work experience. If you want to change careers, have been out of the workforce, or do not have much related work experience, you might want to use a skills resume (see step 3).

Two sample chronological resumes for the same person follow. The first (figure 2-1) is simple, but it works well because Judith is looking for a job in her present career field, has a good job history, and has related education and training. The second example (figure 2-2) is an improved version of this same resume.

Write Your Resume Using the Instant Resume Worksheet

Now it's time to do your own chronological resume. Use the Instant Resume Worksheet beginning on page 12 to complete each part of your basic chronological resume. Following are tips for completing each section.

Identification

- **Name:** This one seems obvious, but you want to avoid some things. For example, don't use a nickname—you need to present a professional image. Even if you have to modify your name a bit from the way you typically introduce yourself, it might be appropriate.

- **Mailing address:** Don't abbreviate words such as "Street" or "Avenue." Include your ZIP code. If you might move during your job search, get an address at your new location so you appear to be settled there. Ask a relative, friend, or neighbor if you can temporarily use his or her address for your mail, or arrange for a post office box.

- **Phone numbers:** Use a phone number that will be answered professionally throughout your job search. Always include your area code. Including your cell phone number is a good way to ensure that you don't miss any calls. Note in parentheses whether it's a cell phone so that callers know what to expect.

- **E-mail address:** If you don't have an e-mail address, get one for free at Yahoo! or Google. Many employers prefer contacting applicants by e-mail, so this is essential.

Judith J. Jones

115 South Hawthorne Avenue
Chicago, Illinois 66204
cell: (312) 653-9217
email: jj@earth.com

SUMMARY

Administrative professional with eight years of experience in office settings. Responsible worker skilled at a variety of tasks.

EDUCATION AND TRAINING

Acme Business College, Lincoln, IL
Graduate of a one-year business program.

U.S. Army
Financial procedures, accounting functions.

John Adams High School, South Bend, IN
Diploma, business education.

Other: Continuing-education classes and workshops in business communication, spreadsheet and database applications, scheduling systems, and customer relations.

EXPERIENCE

XXXX–present—Claims Processor, Blue Spear Insurance Co., Wilmette, IL.
Process customer medical claims, develop management reports based on created spreadsheets, exceed productivity goals.

XXXX–XXXX—Returned to school to upgrade business and computer skills.
Completed courses in advanced accounting, spreadsheet and database programs, office management, human relations.

XXXX–XXXX—E4, U.S. Army.
Assigned to various stations as a specialist in finance operations. Promoted prior to honorable discharge.

XXXX–XXXX—Sandy's Boutique, Wilmette, IL.
Responsible for counter sales, display design, cash register, and other tasks.

XXXX–XXXX—Held part-time and summer jobs throughout high school.

STRENGTHS AND SKILLS

Reliable, hardworking, and good with people. General ledger, accounts payable, and accounts receivable. Proficient in Microsoft Word, Excel, and Outlook.

Figure 2-1: A Simple Chronological Resume

Judith put her recent business schooling in both the Education and Experience sections. Doing this filled a job gap and allows her to present recent training as equivalent to work experience. This resume includes the extra Personal section, where she presents some special strengths that often are not included in a resume.

Judith J. Jones

115 South Hawthorne Avenue
Chicago, IL 66204

jj@earth.com
(312) 653-9217 (cell)

SUMMARY

Administrative professional with eight years of experience in private and public office settings, particularly in insurance and finance. Highly skilled in a variety of tasks, including office management, word processing, and spreadsheet and database program use.

EDUCATION AND TRAINING

Acme Business College, Lincoln, IL
Completed one-year program in **Professional Office Management.** Achieved GPA in top 30% of class. Courses included word processing, accounting theory and systems, advanced spreadsheet and database applications, graphics design, time management, and supervision.

John Adams High School, South Bend, IN
Graduated with emphasis on **business courses.** Earned excellent grades in all business topics and won top award for word-processing speed and accuracy.

Other: Continuing-education programs at own expense, including business communications, customer relations, computer applications, and sales techniques.

EXPERIENCE

XXXX–present—**Claims Processor, Blue Spear Insurance Company,** Wilmette, IL
Process 50 complex medical insurance claims per day, almost 20% above department average. Created a spreadsheet report process that decreased department labor costs by more than $30,000 a year. Received two merit raises for performance.

XXXX–XXXX—**Returned to business school to gain advanced office skills.**

XXXX–XXXX—**Finance Specialist (E4), U.S. Army**
Systematically processed more than 200 invoices per day from commercial vendors. Trained and supervised eight employees. Devised internal system allowing 15% increase in invoices processed with a decrease in personnel. Managed department with a budget equivalent of more than $350,000 a year. Honorable discharge.

XXXX–XXXX—**Sales Associate promoted to Assistant Manager, Sandy's Boutique,** Wilmette, IL
Made direct sales and supervised four employees. Managed daily cash balances and deposits, made purchasing and inventory decisions, and handled all management functions during owner's absence. Sales increased 25% and profits doubled during tenure.

XXXX–XXXX—**Held various part-time and summer jobs through high school while maintaining GPA 3.0/4.0.** Earned enough to pay all personal expenses, including car insurance. Learned to deal with customers, meet deadlines, work hard, and handle multiple priorities.

STRENGTHS AND SKILLS

Reliable, with strong work ethic. Excellent interpersonal, written, and oral communication and math skills. Accept supervision well, effectively supervise others, and work well as a team member. General ledger, accounts payable, and accounts receivable expertise. Proficient in Microsoft Word, Excel, PowerPoint, and Outlook.

Figure 2-2: An Improved Chronological Resume

This improved version adds a number of features, including a more thorough summary, a Strengths and Skills section, and more accomplishments and skills. Notice the impact of the numbers added to this resume, such as "top 30% of class" and "decreased department labor costs by more than $30,000 a year."

Summary

Although you could put together a simple resume without a summary, it is wise to include one. A summary puts your best qualifications at the top and enables you to make your job objective clear. It should emphasize your skills. Here's how Judith Jones presented her summary in her basic resume (figure 2-1):

> *Administrative professional with eight years of experience in office settings. Responsible worker skilled at a variety of tasks.*

Her improved resume's summary says even more:

> *Administrative professional with eight years of experience in private and public office settings, particularly in insurance and finance. Highly skilled in a variety of tasks, including office management, word processing, and spreadsheet and database program use.*

Resume experts often advise job seekers not to include a section titled "Objective," especially on a professional chronological resume. Such statements tend to emphasize what the person wants but do not provide information on what he or she can do. In step 3 I show you how to write an objective for a skills resume that focuses on what you offer rather than what you want.

Use the following worksheet to help you construct an effective and accurate Summary statement for your resume.

THE SUMMARY WORKSHEET

1. **What sort of position, title, and area of specialization do you want?** Write the type of job you want.

   _____

   _____

2. **How many years of related experience do you have altogether?**

   _____

3. **Name any specific areas of expertise or strong interest that you want to use in your next job.** If you have substantial interest, experience, or training in a specific area and want to include it in your summary (remembering that it might limit your options), write it here.

   _____

   _____

(continued)

(continued)

---

4. **Name the key skills you have that are important in this job.** Describe the two or three key skills that are particularly important for success in the job that you are seeking. Select one or more of these that you are strong in and that you enjoy using. Write them here.

_____

_____

The sample resumes throughout this book include summaries that you can review to see how others have phrased them. Browse these for ideas. Now jot down your own draft summary and refine it until it feels right.

Education and Training

Recent graduates or those with good credentials but weak work experience should put their education and training toward the top because it represents a more important part of their experience. More experienced workers with work experience related to their job objective can put their education and training toward the end. Include details of related courses, good grades, related extra-curricular activities, and accomplishments. If it has been a long time since your formal education ended, including recent courses and seminars shows that you are still working to increase your job knowledge and skills.

Work and Volunteer History

This section provides the details of your work history, starting with the most recent job. If you have significant work history, list each job along with details of what you accomplished and special skills you used. Emphasize skills that directly relate to your job objective. Treat volunteer or military experience the same way as other job experiences. This can be very important if this is where you got most of your work experience.

Here are tips for writing your experience listings:

- **Job titles:** You might consider rewording your title to more accurately reflect your responsibilities. Check with your previous supervisors if you are worried about this and ask whether they would object. If you were promoted, you can handle the promotion as a separate job if you need to fill more space.

- **Employers:** Provide the organization's name and list the city and state or province in which it was located. A street address or supervisor's name is not necessary; you can provide those details on a separate sheet of references.

- **Dates:** If you have large employment gaps that are not easily explained, use full years instead of months and years to avoid emphasizing the gaps. If there was a significant period when you did not work, did you do anything that could explain it in a positive way, such as school, travel, or self-employment?

- **Duties and accomplishments:** Include one sentence stating your job description. Follow this with bullets beginning with action verbs (such as *managed, overhauled,* and *created*) that emphasize what you accomplished. Quantify what you did and provide evidence that you did it well. Take particular care to mention skills that directly relate to doing well in the job you want now.

If your previous jobs are not directly related to what you want to do now, emphasize skills you've used that could be used in the new job. For example, someone who waits tables has to deal with people and work quickly under pressure—skills that are needed in many other jobs.

> *T*
> *i*
> *p*
> Look up the descriptions of jobs you have held in the past and jobs you want now in a book titled the Occupational Outlook Handbook. This book is available in most libraries. These descriptions will tell you the skills needed to succeed in the new job. Emphasize these and similar skills in your resume.

Professional Organizations

This is an optional section where you can list job-related professional, humanitarian, or other groups with which you've been involved. These activities might be worth mentioning, particularly if you were an officer or were active in some other way. Mention accomplishments or awards.

Recognition and Awards

If you have received any formal recognition or awards that support your job objective, consider mentioning them. If you have three or more, you can create a separate section for them; otherwise, put them in the Work Experience, Skills, Education, or Personal section.

References

It is not necessary to include the names of your references on a resume or even state "references available on request" at the bottom of your resume. If an employer wants your references, he or she will ask you for them. Be sure that you have asked permission of three references who will give you strong recommendations. Have their contact information available on a separate page to send to employers if they ask for it.

Because some employers have policies against giving references over the phone, ask yours to write a letter of reference for you.

INSTANT RESUME WORKSHEET

Identification

Name _____

Home address _____

ZIP code _____

Phone number and description _____
_____

Alternate phone number and description _____
_____

E-mail address _____

Your Summary

_____
_____
_____
_____
_____
_____

Education and Training

Highest Level/Most Recent Education or Training

Institution name _____

City, state/province (optional) _____

Certificate or degree _____

Specific courses or programs that relate to your job objective _____

_____

_____

Related awards, achievements, and extracurricular activities _____

_____

_____

Anything else that might support your job objective, such as good grades _____

_____

_____

_____

_____

College/Post High School

Institution name _____

City, state/province (optional) _____

Certificate or degree _____

_____

Specific courses or programs that relate to your job objective _____

_____

_____

Related awards, achievements, and extracurricular activities _____

_____

_____

Anything else that might support your job objective, such as good grades _____

_____

_____

_____

_____

High School

Institution name _____

City, state/province (optional) _____

(continued)

Quick Resume Guide

Certificate or degree _____

Specific courses or programs that relate to your job objective _____

_____

_____

Related awards, achievements, and extracurricular activities _____

_____

_____

Anything else that might support your job objective, such as good grades _____

_____

_____

_____

_____

Armed Services Training and Other Training or Certification

Institution name _____

Specific courses or programs that relate to your job objective _____

_____

_____

Related awards, achievements, and extracurricular activities _____

_____

_____

Anything else that might support your job objective, such as good grades _____

_____

_____

_____

_____

Related Workshops, Seminars, Informal Learning, or Any Other Training

_____

_____

_____

_____

_____

_____

Work Experience

Most Recent Position

Dates: from _____ to _____

Organization name _____

City, state/province _____

Your job title(s) _____

Duties _____

Accomplishments _____

_____

_____

Skills _____

_____

_____

Equipment or software you used _____

_____

_____

Next Most Recent Position

Dates: from _____ to _____

Organization name _____

City, state/province _____

Your job title(s) _____

Duties _____

Accomplishments _____

_____

_____

(continued)

Skills _____

_____

_____

Equipment or software you used _____

_____

_____

Next Most Recent Position

Dates: from _____ to _____

Organization name _____

City, state/province _____

Your job title(s) _____

Duties _____

Accomplishments _____

_____

_____

Skills _____

_____

_____

Equipment or software you used _____

_____

_____

Next Most Recent Position

Dates: from _____ to _____

Organization name _____

City, state/province _____

Your job title(s) _____

Duties _____

Accomplishments _____

_____

_____

Skills _____

_____

_____

Equipment or software you used _____

_____

_____

Other Work or Volunteer Experience

_____

_____

_____

_____

Professional Organizations

_____

_____

Pull It Together

At this point you should have completed the Instant Resume Worksheet. Carefully review dates, addresses, phone numbers, spelling, and other details. Transfer this information to a word processing file. Newer versions of Microsoft Word enable you to access dozens of resume templates that can help you put the information into a good-looking format. Then be sure to carefully review it several times to get rid of any typographical errors.

STEP 3: Create a Skills Resume in Just a Few Hours

This step shows you how to write a resume that is organized around the key skills you have that the job you want requires. Although a skills resume requires more time to write than a chronological resume, its advantages might make writing one worthwhile.

In its simplest form, a chronological resume is little more than a list of job titles and other details. Employers often look for candidates with a work history that fits the position. If they want to hire a cost accountant, they will look for someone who has done this work. If you are a recent graduate or have little experience in the career or at the level you now want, you will find that a simple chronological resume emphasizes your *lack* of related experience rather than your ability to do the job.

A skills resume avoids these problems by highlighting what you have done under specific skills headings rather than under past jobs. If you hitchhiked across the country for two years, a skills resume won't necessarily display this as an employment gap. Instead, you could say "Traveled extensively throughout the country and am familiar with most major market areas." That could be very useful experience for certain positions.

> **T i p**
>
> *Because skills resumes can hide your problems, some employers do not like them. But many do. If a chronological resume highlights a weakness, a skills resume might help get you an interview instead of getting screened out.*

Even if you don't have anything to hide, a skills resume emphasizes your key skills and experiences more clearly. And you can always include a chronological list of jobs as one part of your skills resume, as shown in some of this book's examples.

Following is a basic skills resume (figure 3-1). The example is for a recent high school graduate whose only paid work experience has been in fast food. It's a good example of how a skills resume can help someone who does not have the best credentials. It allows the job seeker to present school and extracurricular activities to good effect. It is a strong format choice because it lets her highlight strengths without emphasizing her limited work experience. It doesn't say where she worked or for how long, yet it gives her a shot at many jobs.

Although the sample resume is simple, it presents Lisa in a positive way. She is looking for an entry-level job in a nontechnical area, so many employers will be more interested in her skills than in her job-specific experience. What work experience she does have is presented as a plus. And notice how she listed her gymnastics experience at the bottom.

Lisa M. Rhodes

813 Lava Court • Denver, Colorado 81613
Home: (413) 643-2173 (leave message)
Cell phone: (413) 442-1659
E-mail: lrhodes@netcom.net

Position Desired

Sales-oriented position in a retail sales or distribution business.

Skills and Abilities

Communications	Good written and verbal presentation skills. Use proper grammar and have a good speaking voice.
Interpersonal	Able to get along well with coworkers and accept supervision. Received positive evaluations from previous supervisors.
Flexible	Willing to try new things and am interested in improving efficiency on assigned tasks.
Attention to Detail	Concerned with quality. My work is typically orderly and attractive. Like to see things completed correctly and on time.
Hardworking	Throughout high school, worked long hours in strenuous activities while attending school full-time. Often handled as many as 65 hours a week in school and other structured activities while maintaining above-average grades.
Customer Contacts	Routinely handled as many as 500 customer contacts a day (10,000 per month) in a busy retail outlet. Averaged a lower than .001% complaint rate and was given the "Employee of the Month" award in my second month of employment. Received two merit increases. Never absent or late.
Cash Sales	Handled over $2,000 a day ($40,000 a month) in cash sales. Balanced register and prepared daily sales summaries and deposits.
Reliable	Excellent attendance record, trusted to deliver daily cash deposits totaling more than $40,000 a month.

Education

Franklin High School. Took advanced English and other classes. Member of award-winning band. Excellent attendance record. Superior communication skills. Graduated in top 30% of class.

Other

Active gymnastics competitor for four years. This taught me discipline, teamwork, how to follow instructions, and hard work. I am ambitious, outgoing, reliable, and willing to work.

Figure 3-1: A Basic Skills Resume

Write Your Objective

If you do the activities in step 2 (particularly the Instant Resume Worksheet on page 12), you'll have most of the material you need for the rest of your skills resume. The last things you need to develop are your objective and your skills section.

Although a simple chronological resume does not require a career objective, a skills resume does. Without a reasonably clear job objective, you can't select and organize the key skills you have to support that job objective.

The job objective statement on a skills resume should answer the following questions:

- **What sort of position, title, or area of specialization do you seek?** Is your objective too narrow and specific? Is it so broad or vague that it's meaningless? It's important to be specific but not so specific that you cut yourself out of consideration for other similar jobs that you might fit.

- **What level of responsibility interests you?** Job objectives often indicate a level of responsibility, particularly for supervisory or management roles. If in doubt, always try to keep open the possibility of getting a job with a higher level of responsibility (and, often, salary) than your previous or current one. Write your job objective to include this possibility.

- **What are your most important skills?** What are the two or three most important skills or personal characteristics needed to succeed on the job you're targeting? These are often mentioned in a job objective.

Be careful that your objective tells what you offer rather than what you want. For example, an objective that says "Interested in a position that allows me to be creative and that offers adequate pay and advancement opportunities" is not good. It displays a self-centered, "gimme" approach that will turn off most employers.

Following are a few examples of better job objectives:

> Responsible general-office position in the transportation industry.

> Computer programmer/systems analyst with an accounting emphasis.

> High-volume sales position requiring a success-oriented and aggressive professional.

Write the Skills Section

The most important and unique section of this type of resume is the skills section. This section can be called Areas of Accomplishment, Summary of Qualifications, Areas of Expertise and Ability, and so on. To construct it, you must carefully consider which skills you want to emphasize. Your task is to feature the skills that are essential to success on the job you want *and* that you have and want to use. You probably have a good idea of which skills meet both criteria.

Note that some resumes in this book emphasize skills that are not specific to a particular job. For example, "well organized" is an important skill in many jobs. In your resume, you should provide specific examples of situations or accomplishments that show you possess such skills. You can do this by including examples from previous work or other experiences.

The Key Skills List

Following is a list of skills that are considered key for success on most jobs. It is based on research with employers about the skills they look for in employees. So if you have to emphasize some skills over others, include these.

Key Skills Needed for Success in Most Jobs

Basic Skills Considered the Minimum to Keep a Job	*Key Transferable Skills That Transfer from Job to Job and Are Most Likely Needed in Jobs with Higher Pay and Responsibility*
Basic academic skills	Instruct others
Accept supervision	Manage money and budgets
Follow instructions	Manage people
Get along well with coworkers	Meet the public
Meet deadlines	Work effectively as part of a team
Good attendance	Negotiating
Punctual	Organize/manage projects
Hardworking	Public speaking
Productive	Written and oral communication
Honest	Organizational effectiveness and leadership
	Self-motivation and goal setting
	Creative thinking and problem solving

In addition to the skills on the list, most jobs require skills specific to a particular job. For example, an accountant needs to know how to set up a general ledger, use accounting software, and develop income and expense reports. These job-specific skills are called *job-related skills* and can be quite important in qualifying for a job.

The following worksheet helps you identify your own key skills.

IDENTIFY YOUR KEY SKILLS

Look over the preceding key skills list and write down any skills you have and that are particularly important for the job you want. Add other skills you possess that you feel must be communicated to an employer to get the job you want. Write at least three, but no more than six, of these most important skills:

1. _____

2. _____

3. _____

4. _____

5. _____

6. _____

Prove Your Key Skills with a Story

Now, write each skill you listed in the preceding box on a separate sheet. For each skill, write several detailed examples of when you used it. If possible, you should use work situations, but you can use other situations such as volunteer work, school activities, or other life experiences. Try to quantify the examples by giving numbers such as money saved, sales increased, or other measures to support those skills. Emphasize results you achieved and any accomplishments. Here's an example:

Key skill: Meeting deadlines

I volunteered to help my social organization raise money. I found out about special government funds, but the proposal deadline was only 24 hours away. So I stayed up all night and submitted it on time. We were one of only three groups whose proposals were approved and we were awarded more than $100,000 to fund a youth program for a whole year.

If you carefully consider the skills needed in the preceding story, there are quite a few. Here are some I came up with:

- Hard work
- Meeting deadlines
- Willing to help others
- Good written communication skills
- Persuasive
- Problem solver

Review each "proof sheet" and select the proofs that are particularly valuable in supporting your job objective. You should have at least two proof stories for each skill area. After you select your proofs, rewrite them using action words and short sentences. In the margins, write the skills you needed to do these things. When you're done, write statements you can use in your resume. Rewrite your proof statements and delete anything that does not reinforce the key skills you want to support.

Following is a rewrite of the proof story example. Edit each of your own proofs until they are clear, short, and powerful. You can then use these statements in your resume, modifying them as needed.

Key skill: Meeting deadlines

Submitted a complex proposal on 24-hour notice, successfully obtaining more than $100,000 in funding.

You could easily use this same proof story to support other skills I listed earlier, such as hard work. So, as you write and revise your proof stories, consider which key skills they best support. Use the proofs to support those key skills in your resume.

STEP 4: Develop a Cover Letter and Other Job Search Correspondence

This step provides advice on writing cover letters, JIST Cards, and thank-you notes. It includes various samples of each type of correspondence.

Cover Letters

It is not appropriate to send a resume to someone without explaining why. It is traditional to provide a letter along with your resume—a cover letter. Depending on the circumstances, the letter would explain your situation and ask the recipient for some specific action, consideration, or response.

Writing a simple cover letter *is* pretty simple. Once you know how it's done, you should be able to write one in about 15 minutes or so.

If you think about it, you will send a resume and cover letter to only two groups of people: People you know and people you don't know. This observation makes it easier to understand how to structure your letters to each group. First let's review some basics regarding writing cover letters in general.

Seven Quick Tips for Writing a Superior Cover Letter

No matter whether you know the person you are writing to, virtually every good cover letter should follow these guidelines:

1. **Write to someone in particular.** *Never* send a cover letter "To whom it may concern" or use some other impersonal opening. If you don't send your letter to someone by name, it will be treated like junk mail.

2. **Make absolutely no errors.** One way to offend people quickly is to misspell their names or use incorrect titles. If you have any question, call to verify the correct spelling of the name and other details before you send the letter. Also, review your letters carefully to be sure that they contain no typographical, grammatical, or factual errors.

3. **Personalize your content.** If you can't personalize your letter in some way, don't send it. Form letters never fool anyone. Although some books recommend that you send out lots of these "broadcast letters" to people you don't know, doing so wastes time and money.

4. **Present a good appearance.** Your contacts with prospective employers should always be professional, so use the same good-quality stationery and matching envelopes that you use for the resume. Cover letters are typically printed on standard-size paper; however, you can also use the smaller Monarch-size paper. For colors, stick to white, ivory, or light beige. Use a standard letter format that complements your resume type and format. Most word-processing software provides templates to automate your letter's format and design. And don't forget the envelope! Address it carefully, without abbreviations or errors.

5. **Provide a friendly opening.** Begin your letter with a reminder of any prior contacts and the reason for your correspondence now. The examples later in this section will give you some ideas on how to handle this.

6. **Target your skills and experiences.** To do this well, you must know something about the organization or person with whom you are dealing. Present any relevant background that might be of particular interest to the person to whom you are writing.

7. **Close with an action statement.** Don't close your letter without clearly identifying what you will do next. Don't leave it up to the employer to contact you because that doesn't guarantee a response. Close on a positive note and let the employer know you will make further contact.

Writing Cover Letters to People You Know

It is always best if you know the person to whom you are writing. Written correspondence is less effective than personal contact, so the ideal circumstance is to send a resume and cover letter after having spoken with the person directly. You can come to know people through the Yellow Pages, personal referrals, and other ways. You might not have known them yesterday, but you can get to know them today.

The Four Types of Cover Letters to People You Know

You will be in one of four basic situations when you send cover letters to people you know. Each situation requires a different approach.

1. **An interview is scheduled and a specific job opening might interest you.** The cover letter should provide details of your experience that relate to the specific job.

2. **An interview is scheduled but no specific job is available.** You will send this letter for an interview with an employer who does not have a specific opening now but who might in the future. This is how you find job leads where no one else might be looking.

3. **An interview has taken place.** Many people overlook the importance of sending a letter after an interview. This is a time to say that you want the job and add details on why you can do the job well.

4. **No interview is scheduled yet.** In some situations you just can't arrange an interview before you send a resume and cover letter. In these cases, sending a good cover letter and resume will make later contacts more effective.

Richard Swanson
113 South Meridian
Greenwich, Connecticut 11721

March 10, XXXX

Mr. William Hines
New England Power and Light Company
604 Waterway Boulevard
Darien, Connecticut 11716

Dear Mr. Hines:

I am following up on the brief chat we had today by phone. After getting the details on the position you have open, I am certain that it is the kind of job I have been looking for. A copy of my resume is enclosed providing more details of my background. I hope you have a chance to review it before we meet next week.

My special interest has long been in the large-volume order processing systems that your organization has developed so well. While in school, I researched the flow of order processing work for a large corporation as part of a class assignment. With some simple and inexpensive procedural changes I recommended, check-processing time was reduced by an average of three days. For the number of checks and dollars involved, this one change resulted in an estimated increase in interest revenues of over $35,000 per year.

While I have recently graduated from business school, I have considerable experience for a person of my age. I have worked in a variety of jobs dealing with large numbers of people and deadline pressures. My studies have also been far more "hands-on" and practical than those of most schools, so I have a good working knowledge of current business systems and procedures. This includes a good understanding of various computer spreadsheet and applications programs, the use of automation, and experience with cutting costs and increasing profits. I am also a hard worker and realize I will need to apply myself to get established in my career.

I am most interested in the position you have available and am excited about the potential it offers. I look forward to seeing you next week. If you need to reach me before then, you can call me at (973) 299-3643 or email me at rswanson@msn.net.

Sincerely,

Richard Swanson

Figure 4-1: Pre-interview Cover Letter for a Specific Job Opening

This writer called first and arranged an interview, which is the best approach of all. Note how this new graduate included a specific example of how he saved money for a business by changing its procedures. Although it is not clear from the letter, he gained his experience with people by working as a waiter. Note also how he included skills such as "hard worker" and "deadline pressure."

Writing Cover Letters to People You Don't Know

If it is not practical to directly contact a prospective employer by phone or some other method, it is acceptable to send a resume and cover letter. This approach makes sense in some situations, such as if you are moving to a distant location or responding to a blind ad that offers only a post-office box number. Try to find something you have in common with the person you are contacting. By mentioning this link, your letter then becomes a very personal request for assistance. The letter that follows is an example of how to do this.

John Andrews

January 17, XXXX

The Morning Sun
Box N4317
2 Early Drive
Toronto, Ontario R5C 153

Re: Receptionist/Bookkeeper Position

As I plan on relocating to Toronto, your advertisement for a Receptionist/Bookkeeper caught my attention. Your ad stated yours is a small office and that is precisely what I am looking for. I like dealing with people, and in a previous position, had over 5,000 customer contacts a month. With that experience, I have learned to handle things quickly and pleasantly.

The varied activities in a position combining bookkeeping and reception sound very interesting. I have received formal training in accounting methods and am familiar with accounts receivable, accounts payable, and general ledger posting. I am familiar with several computerized accounting programs and can quickly learn any others that you may be using.

My resume is enclosed for your consideration. Note that I went to school in Toronto and I plan on returning there soon to establish my career. Several members of my family also live there and I have provided their local phone number, should you wish to contact me. Please contact that number as soon as possible, since I plan on being in Toronto in the near future and would like to speak with you about this or future positions with your company. I will call you in the next few weeks to set up an appointment should I not hear from you before then.

Thank you in advance for your consideration in this matter.

Sincerely,

12 Lake Street
Chicago, Illinois 60631
587.488.3876
johnandrews@cincore.com

John Andrews

P.S. You can reach me via email at johnandrews@cincore.com or leave a phone message at 587.488.3876.

Figure 4-2: Response to a Want Ad

Responding to a want ad puts you in direct competition with the many others who will read the same ad, so the odds are not good that this letter would get a response. The fact that the writer does not yet live in the area is another negative. Still, I believe that you should follow up on any legitimate lead you find. In this case, someone who is available to interview right away will likely fill the position. But a chance exists that, with good follow-up, another position will become available. Or the employer might be able to give the writer the names of others to contact.

The Hardworking JIST Card®

JIST Cards are a job search tool that gets results. I developed JIST Cards in the early 1970s, almost by accident. I was surprised by the positive employer reaction but paid attention and developed them further. Over the years, I have seen them in every imaginable format, and forms of JIST Cards are being used on the Internet, in personal video interviews, and in other electronic media.

A JIST Card is carefully constructed to contain all the essential information most employers want to know in a very short format:

- Name, phone number, and e-mail address
- The type of position you seek
- Your experience, education, and training
- Key job-related skills, performance, and results
- Your good-worker traits
- Any special conditions you are willing to work under (optional)

A JIST Card typically uses a 3×5 card format but has been designed into many other sizes and formats, such as a folded business card. It can be as simple as handwritten or done with graphics and on special papers. You should create JIST Cards in addition to a resume because you will use your JIST Cards in a different way.

JIST Cards get results. In my surveys of employers, over 90 percent form a positive impression of the JIST Card's writer within 30 seconds. More amazing is that about 80 percent of employers say they would be willing to interview the person behind the JIST Card, even if they did not have a job opening at the time.

You can use a JIST Card in many ways, including the following:

- Attached to your resume or application
- Enclosed in a thank-you note
- Given to your friends, relatives, and other contacts—so that they can give them to other people
- Sent out to everyone who graduated from your school or who are members of a professional association
- Put on car windshields

- Posted on the supermarket bulletin board
- On the Internet, in addition to resume content

Many office-supply stores have perforated light card stock sheets that you can use in your printer. Many word-processing programs have templates that allow you to format a 3×5-inch card. You can also use regular-size paper, print several cards on a sheet, and cut it to the size you need. The point is to get lots of them in circulation. The following sample JIST Cards use a plain format, but you can make them as fancy as you want.

Sandy Nolan

Position: General Office/Clerical

Message: (512) 232-9213

More than two years of work experience plus one year of training in office practices. Type 55 wpm, trained in word processing, post general ledger, interpersonal skills, and get along with most people. Can meet deadlines and handle pressure well.

Willing to work any hours

Organized, honest, reliable, and hardworking

Richard Straightarrow   Home: (602) 253-9678
                                   Message: (602) 257-6643

Objective: Electronics installation, maintenance, and sales

Four years of work experience plus two-year AA degree in Electronics Engineering Technology. Managed a $360,000/year business while going to school full time, with grades in the top 25%. Familiar with all major electronic diagnostic and repair equipment. Hands-on experience with medical, consumer, communication, and industrial electronics equipment and applications. Good problem-solving and communication skills. Customer-service oriented.

Willing to do what it takes to get the job done

Self motivated, dependable, learn quickly

Juanita Rodriguez   Message: (639) 361-1754

Position: Warehouse Management

Six years of experience plus two years of formal business course work. Have supervised a staff as large as 16 people and warehousing operations covering more than two acres and valued at over $14,000,000. Automated inventory operations resulting in a 30% increase in turnover and estimated annual savings of more than $250,000. Working knowledge of accounting, computer systems, time & motion studies, and advanced inventory-management systems.

Will work any hours

Responsible, hardworking, and can solve problems

Thank-You Notes

Although resumes and cover letters get the attention, thank-you notes often get results. Sending thank-you notes makes both good manners and good job search sense. When used properly, thank-you notes can help you create a positive impression with employers that more formal correspondence often can't. Here are some situations when you should use them:

1. **Before an interview:** In some situations, you can send a less formal note before an interview. For example, you can simply thank someone for being willing to see you. Depending on the situation, enclosing a resume could be a bit inappropriate. Remember, this is supposed to be sincere thanks for help and not an assertive business situation.

2. **After an interview:** One of the best times to send a thank-you note is right after an interview. In addition to making a positive impression, it creates yet another opportunity for you to remain in the employer's consciousness at an important time. Send a thank-you note right after the interview and certainly within 24 hours.

3. **Whenever anyone helps you in your job search:** This includes those who give you referrals, people who provide advice, or simply those who are supportive during your search. Enclose one or more JIST Cards in these notes because recipients can give them to others who might be in a better position to help you.

Following is an example of a thank-you note.

Sample Thank-You Note

August 11, XXXX

Dear Mr. O'Beel,

Thank you for the opportunity to interview for the position available in your production department. I want you to know that this is the sort of job I have been looking for and that I am enthusiastic about the possibility of working for you.

I believe that I have both the experience and skills to fit nicely into your organization and to be productive quickly.

Thanks again for the interview; I enjoyed the visit.

Sara Smith

(505) 665-0090

Seven Quick Tips for Writing Thank-You Notes

Here are some brief tips to help you write your thank-you notes:

1. **Use quality paper and envelopes.** Use good-quality notepaper with matching envelopes. Most stationery stores have thank-you note cards and envelopes in a variety of styles. Select a note that is simple and professional—avoid cute graphics and sayings. A simple "Thank You" on the front will do. For a professional look, match your resume and thank-you note papers by getting them at the same time. I suggest off-white and buff colors.

2. **Handwritten or typed is acceptable.** Traditionally, thank-you notes are handwritten. If your handwriting is good, it is perfectly acceptable to write them. If not, they can be word-processed.

3. **Use a formal salutation.** Unless you know the person you are thanking, don't use a first name. Write "Dear Ms. Pam Smith," "Ms. Smith," or "Dear Ms. Smith" rather than the less formal "Dear Pam." Include the date.

4. **Keep the note short and friendly.** This is not the place to write "The reason you should hire me is…." Remember, the note is a thank-you for what someone else did, not a hard-sell pitch for what you want. And make sure it doesn't sound like a form letter. As appropriate, be specific about when you will next contact the person. Make sure that you include something to remind the employer of who you are and how to reach you because your name alone might not be enough to be remembered.

5. **Sign it.** Sign your first and last name. Avoid initials and make your signature legible.

6. **Send it right away.** Write and send your note no later than 24 hours after you make your contact. Ideally, you should write it immediately after the contact, while the details are fresh in your mind.

7. **Enclose a JIST Card.** Depending on the situation, a JIST Card is often the ideal enclosure. It's small, soft sell, and provides your phone number. It is a reminder of you, should any jobs open up, and a tool to pass along to someone else. Make sure your thank-you notes and envelopes are big enough to enclose an unfolded JIST Card.

STEP 5: Use Your Resume on the Internet

Although the Internet has helped many people find job leads, far more have been disappointed. The problem is that many job seekers assume they can simply put resumes in Internet resume databases and employers will line up to hire them. It sometimes happens this way, but not often. This is the same negative experience that people have when sending lots of unsolicited resumes to personnel offices—a hopeful but mostly ineffective approach that was around long before computers.

As with sending out many unsolicited resumes, putting your resume on the Internet is a passive approach that is unlikely to work well for you. Instead, think of Internet resumes as a tool to facilitate your active networking and job search efforts.

Converting Your Resume to Electronic Formats

When you post your resume to an online resume database such as Monster or that of a particular hiring company, it could be stored as a text file with no graphics or other fancy formatting. Employers search these text files for keywords that match their requirements for the jobs they have open. What this means is that your resume's carefully done format and design elements could get stripped out when you upload it. So, you are better off simplifying the format yourself before distributing your resume online.

Look at the sample partial resume that follows, which was written by Susan Britton Whitcomb and featured in her book *Résumé Magic*. This resume has had all formatting and graphic elements removed for submission in electronic form. It has the following features:

- No graphics
- No lines (it uses equal signs instead)
- No bold, italic, or other text variations
- Only one common font (Courier in this case)
- No tab indents
- No line or paragraph indents

```
AMY RICCIUTI
776 Whiting Lane
Greenville, ME 00247
(203) 433-3322
aricciuti@email.com

PROFESSIONAL EXPERIENCE
================================================================

ROCKWOOD INSURANCE, Augusta, ME
[year]-Present

Independent agency specializing in commercial coverage for
transportations and lumber industries.

Underwriting manager. . .

Recruited by partner/sales manager to manage underwriting in support
of aggressive expansion/business development campaign. Liaison to 5
agents and some 50 companies. Underwrite $6 million in renewal
coverage and $200,000 in new business on a priority basis (commercial
and personal lines). Collaborate with agents to protect loss ratios.
Maintain knowledge of company submission standards and acceptability
of accounts. Aggressively process submissions to meet critical
deadlines and offer better premium to customers.
```

```
*** Contributions ***

+ Assisted with AMS Novell network upgrade (resident expert for software
installation, troubleshooting).

+ Took on several new books of business during tenure without need for
additional support staff.


BURRELL INSURANCE, Oklahoma City, OK
[year] - [year]

Customer Service Representative (Commercial Lines) for primary oil
field-related clients (equipment maintenance, drilling, oil field
contracting, welding, wrought iron erection, construction).


EDUCATION, LICENSURE
=================================================================

INS 21 (Principles of Insurance), INS 23(Commercial Principles of
Insurance), Personal Lines (Property and Auto), Commercial Lines
(Property), E&O Coverage, Employee Practice Liability, Property &
Casualty Agent (#760923)
```

Figure 5-1: A Plain-Text Resume

You can easily take your existing resume and reformat it for electronic submission. Here are some quick guidelines to do so:

- Copy and paste your resume text into a new file in your word processor.

- Eliminate graphic elements such as lines or images.

- Set the margins to no more than 65 characters wide.

- Use a common font, such as Courier or Times New Roman. Eliminate bold, italic, and other styles.

- Introduce major sections with words in all uppercase letters, rather than in bold or a different font.

- Keep all text left-aligned.

- Use standard keyboard characters, such as the asterisk in place of bullets.

- Instead of using the tab key or paragraph indents, use the spacebar to indent.

When you're done, click the File menu and the Save As command. Then select the Plain Text, ASCII (American Standard Code for Information Interchange), or Text Only option from the Save As Type box. Then give the file a different name and click Save or OK. Then reopen the file to see how it looks. Make any additional format changes as needed, such as rebreaking lines or adding line spaces. Close the document and reopen it in a text editor, such as Notepad or TextEdit (Mac OS X), to double-check that all of the characters have been converted correctly.

The Importance of Keywords

Creating an electronic resume is more involved than just putting it into a plain format. Employers look for qualified applicants in a resume database by searching for keywords. Your task is to add the right keywords to your electronic resume so that your chance of being selected for appropriate jobs is increased.

You will want to use keywords to make your resume match employers' job ads as closely as possible. In addition to using words directly from the job posting, try these tactics:

- **Think like a prospective employer.** Think of the jobs you want, and then include the keywords you think an employer would use to find someone who can do what you can do.

- **Review job descriptions from major references.** Read the descriptions for the jobs you seek in major references such as the *Occupational Outlook Handbook* (www.bls.gov/oco).

- **Include all your important skill words.** Include the key skills you documented in step 3.

- **Look for additional sources of keywords to include.** You can identify keywords by reviewing the sample resumes in the appendix, descriptions of jobs you want, want ads, employer Web sites, job board postings, and more.

Using Your Resume Online

Now you are ready to apply for jobs using your electronic resume. One way you might do this is through a company's Web site. Some employer sites ask you to submit your resume by copying it from your file and pasting it into boxes on the Web site. Others ask you to upload your resume file directly to their database from a Word file. Be sure to read and follow the directions carefully for each site. Many will ask you to set up an account on the site before you can upload your resume and apply for jobs. Some will even send you e-mail alerts if a job comes up that matches your experience.

If you are sending your resume to an employer via e-mail, a good practice is to copy and paste the text/ASCII version into the body of your e-mail message, right after an introductory letter. If the employer will accept attachments, also attach your resume as a PDF or Word file, depending on the employer's preferences. PDF (Portable Document Format) files, which are created using Adobe Acrobat, preserve your formatting and allow hiring managers to print an attractive version of your resume.

It doesn't hurt to upload your resume to general and career-specific job banks, too, in hopes of being found by a company or recruiter. Just be aware that doing so leaves you open for spam and scams, so judge the responses carefully. And don't count on passively putting your resume on these sites to get you a job. It's a long shot.

Best Resume Banks and Job Boards

These Web sites provide listings of job openings and allow you to add your resume for employers to look at. All allow you to look up job openings in a variety of useful ways, including location, job type, and other criteria. Most get their fees from employers and don't charge job seekers.

- **BestJobsUSA.com:** www.bestjobsusa.com
- **CareerBuilder:** www.careerbuilder.com
- **JobBankUSA.com:** www.jobbankusa.com
- **Monster:** www.monster.com
- **NationJob:** www.nationjob.com
- **NicheBoards.com:** www.nicheboards.com
- **Simply Hired:** www.simplyhired.com
- **TheLadders:** www.theladders.com
- **Vault:** www.vault.com
- **Yahoo! HotJobs:** http://hotjobs.yahoo.com/

Blogs, Online Portfolios, and Networking Sites

With thanks to Kirsten Dixson and Lori Cates Hand

Now that you've seen how to format and effectively distribute your resume online, it's also important to understand that others will be using the Internet to find and research you. It's becoming almost standard practice for employers to google applicants at some point during the process, and to screen out those whose online information is unflattering. The best way to combat this is to put up positive information about yourself, in the form of online profiles, portfolios, blogs, and more (and to avoid posting unprofessional information anywhere online).

Your Own Blog

One of the easiest and most economical ways to get an online presence that is well-designed and will come up high in Web searches is to create a professional *blog* (short for *Weblog*). With TypePad (www.typepad.com) or Blogger (www.blogger.com), you don't have to know HTML to start posting articles about your area of expertise. Just make sure that your posts are professional and relevant to your target audience. Use this vehicle to demonstrate your knowledge, experience, and current grasp on happenings in your industry. On your blog, you can make your resume available for download (include text, Word, and PDF versions), link to other relevant sites, and include your career bio on the "about" page.

> **Tip**
>
> *What goes in a career-management blog? There are no rules, but common sense and good writing apply. There have been cases where people have been fired for blogging about proprietary corporate information or making unflattering remarks about their work environment. Ninety percent of your posts should be relevant to your professional target audience. Because blogs are expected to reveal your personality, you should occasionally write about your interests—but only the ones that you'd also include on a resume.*

Social Networking Sites

I highly recommend that you join business networking site LinkedIn (www.linkedin.com) and use it to connect with all the people in your personal and business networks. Fill out the profile section with information from your resume. Include a link to your resume and blog, if you have one. Your LinkedIn profile will come up close to the top in results when people search for you online.

If you are on Twitter (www.twitter.com), use it to pass along information relevant to your industry and show your own expertise. Facebook is a good place to reconnect with old friends who might know of job openings. But because Facebook tends to be more social than professional, be sure to change your privacy settings so that nobody outside your network of friends can access your Facebook postings. Also, avoid posting anything that makes you look bad.

Online Career Portfolios

To give employers a more comprehensive picture of who you are and what you have done, you can create an online career portfolio. A Web portfolio is the traditional paper portfolio concept reinvented for the online medium with links and multimedia content. Portfolios are more than Web-based resumes in that they *must* contain evidence of your past performance, including work samples, testimonials, articles, video, photographs, charts, and so on.

Providing all of this information helps potential employers feel like they know you before they even meet you. The portfolio concept also helps prove the facts on your resume because it shows instead of just telling. Prospective employers and clients want to see that you have solved problems like theirs.

If you say that you have strong presentation skills, show a video clip. Articles, awards, graphs, audio references, white papers, case studies, press releases, and schedules of appearances are just some of the things you can include to prove your expertise.

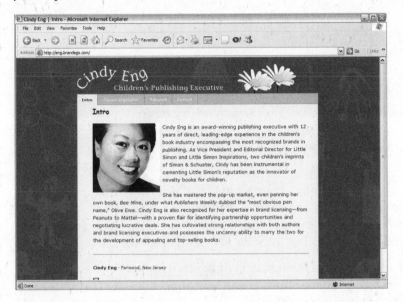

Figure 5-2: A Web Portfolio

Figure 5-2 shows the Web portfolio of Cindy Eng, Vice President and Editorial Director for Scholastic At Home. Says Cindy, "I landed a great new job as a direct result of a networking contact finding my Brandego portfolio and seeing that my background was a perfect match for a position that his executive recruiter was trying to fill. My Web portfolio made it easy to distribute my resume and show examples of projects during my interviews. My new colleagues told me that they were reassured by my qualifications when they googled me after the announcement of my hire. I like that when I'm googled, my portfolio is the first thing that is found."

You can check out more Web portfolio examples at www.brandego.com/gallery.php.

Another option for creating an interactive online portfolio is VisualCV (www.visualcv.com). This site enables you to build a free online portfolio of various elements. Then you can send employers a link to it, or post it alongside your resume in job banks such as Monster and CareerBuilder.

After completing some or all of steps 1 and 2, you are ready to put together a better resume. By better, I mean one that is more carefully crafted than those you have already done. This step will help you pull together what you have learned and create an effective resume. It also expands on tips in step 2 on how to design, produce, and use your resume to best effect.

This step assumes that you have read and done the activities in steps 1, 2, and 3. I also assume that you have done a basic resume as outlined in those steps, and I hope you have taken my advice to use it right away while you worked on creating a better resume as time permitted.

Writing and Editing Tips

You learned to write a basic chronological resume in step 2. Although a traditional chronological resume has limitations, you can add some information and modify its style to your advantage. Here are things you can do, depending on your situation:

- **Emphasize skills and accomplishments.** Most chronological resumes simply provide a listing of tasks, duties, and responsibilities. But you should clearly emphasize skills, accomplishments, and results that support that objective. Use numbers to quantify your results.

- **Expand your Education and Training section.** Let's say that you are a recent graduate who worked your way through school, earned decent grades (while working full time), and was involved in extracurricular activities. The standard listing of education would not do you justice, so consider expanding that section to include statements about your accomplishments while going to school.

- **Add new sections to highlight your strengths.** There is no reason you can't add one or more sections to your resume to highlight something you think will help you. For example, let's say you have excellent references from previous employers. You might add a statement to that effect and even include one or more positive quotes. Or maybe you got exceptional performance reviews, wrote some articles, edited a newsletter, traveled extensively, or did something else that might support your job objective. If so, nothing prevents you from creating a special section or heading to highlight these activities.

- **Create a portfolio.** Some occupations typically require a portfolio of your work or some other concrete example of what you have done. Artists, copywriters, graphic designers, clothing designers, architects, radio and TV personalities, and many others know this and should take care to provide good examples of what they do.

- **As much as possible, write your resume yourself.** Even though I encourage you to borrow ideas from this book's sample resumes, your resume must end up being yours. You have to be able to defend its content and prove every statement you've made. Even if you end up hiring someone to help with your resume, you must provide this person with what to say and let him or her help you with how to say it. However you do it, make sure that your resume is *your* resume and that it represents you accurately.

- **Don't lie or exaggerate.** Some job applicants misrepresent themselves and lie about their education, salaries, responsibilities, or job titles. Don't be tempted. For one reason, it is simply not right. But there are also practical reasons for not doing so. The first is that you might get a job that you can't handle. Another reason is that some employers check references and backgrounds more thoroughly than you might realize. If you are caught, you could lose your job.

- **Never include a negative.** Telling the truth does not mean you have to tell *everything*. Some things are better left unsaid, and a resume should present your strengths and not your weaknesses. For example, if you are competing with people who have a degree and you don't, it is better to not mention your education (or, in this case, lack of it). Instead, emphasize your skills and accomplishments. If you can do the job, lack of education really shouldn't matter, and many employers will hire based on what you can do, rather than on what you don't have.

- **Don't be humble.** Being honest on your resume does not mean you can't present the facts in the most positive way. A resume is not a place to be humble. So work on *what* you say and *how* you say it, so that you present your experiences and skills as positively as possible.

- **Use short sentences and simple words.** Short sentences are easier to read. They communicate better than long ones. Simple words also communicate more clearly than long ones.

- **If it doesn't support your job objective, cut it out.** A resume is only one or two pages long, so you have to be careful what you do and do not include. Review each word and ask yourself, "Does this support my ability to do the job in some clear way?" If not, it should go.

- **Include numbers.** Numbers quantify your results and show what you can do for a company. They could refer to the speed at which someone does word processing, the number of transactions processed per month, the percentage of increased sales, the number of people or orders processed, or some other numerical measure of performance.

- **Emphasize your skills.** In addition to listing the key skills needed to support your job objective in a skills resume, you should include a variety of skill statements in all narrative sections of your resume. In each case, select skills you have that support your job objective.

- **Edit, edit, edit.** Every word has to count in your resume, so keep editing until it is right. This might require you to make multiple passes and to change your resume many times. But, if you did as I suggested and have created a simple but acceptable resume, fretting over your better resume shouldn't delay your job search one bit.

Design Tips

Just as some people aren't good at resume writing, others are not good at design. Many resumes use simple designs, and this is acceptable for most situations. But you can do other things to improve your resume's appearance:

- **Make it more readable.** Use short sentences and short paragraphs. Don't use margins that are too narrow. Be sure to include plenty of white space around the text and between sections.

- **Use strategic placement.** Put important information on the top and to the left because people scan materials from left to right and top to bottom.

- **Keep it simple.** Don't use too many typestyles (fonts) on the same page. Using one or two fonts is ideal; three is pushing it. Use underlining, bold type, and bullets to emphasize and separate information—but use them sparingly.

- **Don't pack it.** Sometimes it's hard to avoid including lots of detail, but doing so can make your resume appear crowded and hard to read. In many cases, you can shorten a crowded resume with good editing, which would allow for considerably more white space.

- **Use two pages if you need to.** One page is often enough if you are disciplined in your editing, but two uncrowded pages are far better than one crowded one. Those with considerable experience or high levels of responsibility often require a two-page resume. If you end up with one-and-a-half pages of resume, add content or white space until it fills both pages.

- **Consider graphics.** Although resumes with extensive graphic design elements are not the focus for this book, some resumes clearly benefit from this. Good graphic design is more important for those in creative jobs such as advertising, art, and desktop publishing.

- **Edit again for appearance.** Just as your resume's text requires editing, you should be prepared to review and make additional changes to your resume's design. After you have written the content just as you want it, you will probably need to make additional editing and design changes so that everything looks right.

Get Help If You Need It

If you are not particularly good at writing and designing a resume, consider getting help with various elements. Several sources of help are available—in particular, professional resume writers.

In reviewing a resume writer's capabilities, you need to have a good idea of the services you want and buy only those you need. For example, some resume writers have substantial experience and skills in career counseling and can help you clarify what you want to do. Helping you write your resume might be the end result of more-expensive, time-consuming career counseling services that you might or might not need. Most professional resume writers ask you questions about your skills, experiences, and accomplishments so that they can use this information to improve your resume. This expertise will benefit almost everyone.

But, in some cases, the writer excels at presenting the information you give them in the most flattering light but expects you to have figured out your career objectives on your own. Simple resume writing should cost less than resume help that comes with career coaching services. Ask for prices and know exactly what is included before you commit to any resume-writing services.

Some resume writers provide additional services. These services include printing a number of resumes and envelopes, giving you the electronic files (to enable you to make future changes), putting your resume into an electronic format for Internet posting, or posting your electronic resume on one or more Internet sites.

You can locate resume writers through the yellow pages under "Resume Service" or similar headings. Also, you can often find their ads in the newspaper's help-wanted section. You can also find them through professional organizations (see the box on the next page). But perhaps the best source is through a referral by someone who has worked with a specific writer, so ask around.

Ask for Credentials

Four major associations of professional resume writers exist: the **Professional Association of Résumé Writers and Career Coaches** (PARW/CC; www.parw.com), the **National Résumé Writers' Association** (NRWA; www.nrwa.com), **Career Directors International** (www.careerdirectors.com), and the **Career Management Alliance** (The Alliance; www.careermanagementalliance.com). These affiliations are often included in Yellow Pages advertisements. Because each of these associations has a code of ethics, someone who belongs to one or more of these groups offers better assurance of legitimate services. Members of these associations wrote many of the sample resumes in the appendix.

Better yet is someone who is a Certified Professional Resume Writer (CPRW), Nationally Certified Resume Writer (NCRW), Certified Resume Writer (CRW), Master Resume Writer (MRW), or similar designation, a process that requires passing resume-writing competency tests. In any situation, ask for the credentials of the person who will provide the service and see examples of the person's work before you agree to anything.

In your search for someone to help you with your resume, you might run into high-pressure efforts to sell you services. If so, buyer beware! Good, legitimate job search and career professionals are out there, and they are worth every bit of their reasonable fees. Many employers pay thousands of dollars for outplacement assistance to help those leaving find new jobs. But some career-counseling businesses prey on unsuspecting, vulnerable souls who are unemployed. Some "packages" can cost thousands of dollars and are not worth the price.

I have said for years that many job seekers would gain more from reading a few good job search books than they might get from the less-than-legitimate businesses offering these services. But how do you tell the legitimate from the illegitimate? One clue is high-pressure sales and high fees. If this is the case, your best bet is to walk out quickly. Call the agency first and get some information on services offered and prices charged. If the agency requires that you come in to discuss this, assume that it is a high-pressure sales outfit and avoid it.

Low-cost services often are available from local colleges or other organizations. These may consist of workshops and access to reading materials, assessment tests, and other services at a modest cost or even free. Consider these as an alternative to higher-priced services.

Appendix

More Sample Resumes and Cover Letters

You can learn a lot by looking at examples of good resumes. Here is a collection of great resumes written by professional resume writers. Thanks to all of them for their excellent contributions.

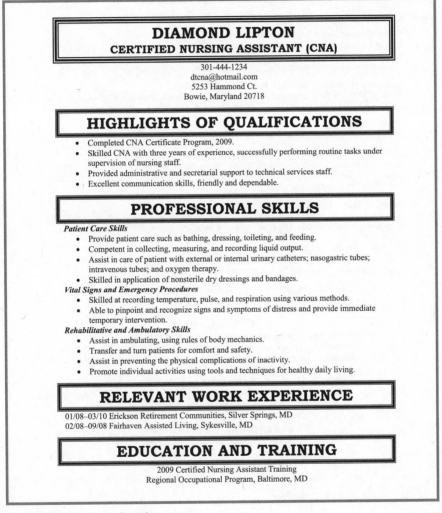

DIAMOND LIPTON
CERTIFIED NURSING ASSISTANT (CNA)

301-444-1234
dtcna@hotmail.com
5253 Hammond Ct.
Bowie, Maryland 20718

HIGHLIGHTS OF QUALIFICATIONS

- Completed CNA Certificate Program, 2009.
- Skilled CNA with three years of experience, successfully performing routine tasks under supervision of nursing staff.
- Provided administrative and secretarial support to technical services staff.
- Excellent communication skills, friendly and dependable.

PROFESSIONAL SKILLS

Patient Care Skills
- Provide patient care such as bathing, dressing, toileting, and feeding.
- Competent in collecting, measuring, and recording liquid output.
- Assist in care of patient with external or internal urinary catheters; nasogastric tubes; intravenous tubes; and oxygen therapy.
- Skilled in application of nonsterile dry dressings and bandages.

Vital Signs and Emergency Procedures
- Skilled at recording temperature, pulse, and respiration using various methods.
- Able to pinpoint and recognize signs and symptoms of distress and provide immediate temporary intervention.

Rehabilitative and Ambulatory Skills
- Assist in ambulating, using rules of body mechanics.
- Transfer and turn patients for comfort and safety.
- Assist in preventing the physical complications of inactivity.
- Promote individual activities using tools and techniques for healthy daily living.

RELEVANT WORK EXPERIENCE

01/08–03/10 Erickson Retirement Communities, Silver Springs, MD
02/08–09/08 Fairhaven Assisted Living, Sykesville, MD

EDUCATION AND TRAINING

2009 Certified Nursing Assistant Training
Regional Occupational Program, Baltimore, MD

Submitted by Brenda Thompson

This resume for a Certified Nursing Assistant uses a simple functional format that highlights skills and recent certification.

William C. Hedges
555 Ridge Road, Princeton, NJ 08540
(609) 921-5555 Work • (609) 921-5566 Fax • billhedges@tgi.com

QUALIFICATIONS
- ☑ **Database Programmer. Computer Programmer**—applications in C/C++ and Java
- ☑ Proactive team player with proven communications and organization talents.
- ☑ Computer skills: C/C++, STL (Standard Template Library), Java (JDK 6), Visual Basic 6, Oracle (SQL, SQL*Plus, PL/SQL), DataEase, Windows Vista/XP/2003, UNIX.

PROFESSIONAL EXPERIENCE

Technical Skills & Programming
- **Point-of-Sales, AR/AP System** for Technology Group, Inc.
  Created a normalized relational database (using DataEase) to provide complete invoicing, billing, and accounts receivable / accounts payable system for $1 million business with 300 active accounts and mailing list of 3,500. Currently running on Windows XP network.

- **Client-Server Sales Module in Java**—Class Project
  Using TCP/IP sockets, connected GUI front end to console application, allowing user to query server for price, availability, and credit status. Provided for simple update functionality.

- **C/C++**—Class Project
  Binary search tree. 2–3 search tree. Quick sort on linked list. String class. STL.

- **Sales Module in Visual Basic Connected to Access Database**—Class Project
  Created GUI front end to Access database (using Visual Basic) allowing input of customer information, part numbers, and quantities; and enabling users to place orders and print invoices and sales summaries.

- **Billing System in Oracle**—Class Project
  Generated users, tables, views, sequences and triggers using SQL, SQL*Plus, and PL/SQL to create Oracle database. Imported data and used Developer 2000 to create forms.

Leadership & Organization Skills
- Spearheaded growth of mail-order business from $50,000 to $700,000 annually. Developed export customers in Europe, Africa, the Middle East, and Australia.

- Provide cross-functional expertise in overseeing daily operations, including technology, accounting, bookkeeping, taxes, purchasing, personnel, marketing, and customer relations.

EDUCATION
Technology Institute of New Jersey, Somerset, NJ—2009 to 2010
Computer Science / Technology Coursework—19 credits, GPA 4.0
Data Structures and Algorithms, C++, Java, Visual Basic, Oracle/SQL, Networking

EMPLOYMENT HISTORY
Owner / General Business Manager, Technology Group, Inc., Princeton, NJ—1997 to present
One of the largest beekeeping supply companies on the East Coast

PROFESSIONAL ASSOCIATIONS
Computing Machinery Professionals Association—CMPA
New Jersey CMPA / TECE Joint Chapter
New Jersey Computer Users Group

Submitted by Susan Guarneri

This resume's summary pinpoints the candidate's career target and highlights his technical skills. He has used class projects as experience. Paid employment is moved close to the end because it's not as relevant to his career goal.

PAULA MARTIN
VETERINARY TECHNICIAN
pmartin@protypeltd.com

889 Westfield Street
Agawam, MA 06001
413.555.7644

Compassionate and competent **Veterinary Technician** with 6+ years of experience assisting veterinarians in medical and surgical procedures, ranging from routine to emergency and critical care. Recognized as efficient; skilled in multitasking; and dedicated to providing prompt, courteous service. Effective communicator who enjoys working with people and animals and is able to educate owners on protecting their companion animals' health and well-being.

PROFESSIONAL EXPERIENCE

VETERINARY TECHNICIAN
Harrington Animal Clinic, Agawam, MA   2000 to Present
Assist 5 veterinarians in providing comprehensive veterinary care. Skilled in performing the following:

Medical & Surgical Procedures
- Assist in all types of medical treatments (and with restraints), ranging from routine office examinations to critical care, emergency situations, euthanasia, and house calls.
- Set up all equipment and prep animals for surgery: shaving, intubating, inserting IV catheters, and administering intravenous/intramuscular drugs.
- Assist with surgeries, including spaying/neutering, exploratory, cystotomy, nasal scope, endoscopy, cruciate/luxating patella, abscess, declawing, and other procedures.
- Prepare and sterilize surgical packs in an autoclave; monitor anesthesia and patients' vital signs. Administer subcutaneous fluids. Perform complete dentistry.
- Accurately document anesthetic drugs used during surgery; handle post-surgical recovery: extubation, patient monitoring, and calling clients to provide follow-up/status reports.
- Prepare vaccines; refill/dispense medications; administer oral medications/vaccines under supervision and provide instructions to clients; assist with administration of chemotherapy.

Tests / Lab Work / Client Education
- Conduct heartworm, Feline Leukemia, and FIV tests. Take glucose and blood (including jugular) samples. Read results of urinalysis and fecal samples.
- Perform and develop radiographs as required. Assist specialists in restraining animals during ultrasounds.
- Educate clients on diseases/preventive care, home care (post surgery, diabetic discharges, and administering subcutaneous fluids and medications), grooming, diet, geriatric care, declawing alternatives, and other aspects of animal health care.
- Groom and bathe animals, including fungal baths, lion clips, and reverse sedation according to veterinarian's instruction.

Front Office / Administration
- Cross-trained to perform front office duties, including scheduling routine health exams and surgical appointments, invoicing/cashing out, providing estimates, and more. Greet clients and set up patients in exam rooms.
- Place orders for medications and various products per veterinarians' instructions. Sell products to clients.
- Utilize customized computer applications to process payments and enter patient records.
- Serve as resource to new technicians by answering questions on equipment, office, and other procedures.

EDUCATION / TRAINING

A.S., Veterinary Technician; BRIARWOOD COLLEGE, Springfield, MA   2000

Additional Training:
Completed intensive on-the-job 3-month training under guidance of licensed veterinarians at Harrington Animal Clinic.

Submitted by Louise Garver

This candidate landed a job from the very first resume she sent out! Her profile reinforces the diverse clinical and soft skills she offers that relate to her objective. Experience is organized within skill headings to reinforce the depth of her knowledge and capabilities to work with a wide range of animals.

45

DONALD JACOBS
Confidential Security Clearance

1200 Peninsula Square
Cleveland, Ohio 44122

Home: (216) 333-1234
djacobs01@yahoo.com

A dedicated Electronics Technician with more than ten years of hands-on experience, with the ability to lead and motivate a diverse crew. Experienced in the utilization of creative problem-solving and solution techniques, while exuding decisive and confident decision-making abilities. Skilled in information systems management, with emphasis in program management, and internal control procedures.

- *Computer Software*—Knowledgeable in MS Word and Excel. Understand C program language and able to perform some software program modifications.
- *Operator Mechanic*—Work closely with engineering personnel to assist in troubleshooting software and hardware using electronic schematics and technical procedures.
- *Quality Assurance*—Write quality reports for non-conformances and repairs conducted.
- *Test Planning*—Plan test environment using required equipment and documentation. Implement test plan with little or no supervision.
- *Troubleshoot and Repair*—Experience with troubleshooting mechanical, electrical, and electronic systems.

EXPERIENCE

AVTRON MANUFACTURING, Independence, OH (2009–Present)
Field Service Engineer
Primary responsibilities include writing service orders, distributing new technical bulletins to the site, training on maintenance practices and scanner operations, coordinating troubleshooting/maintenance with other vendor companies when needed, and assisting technical support group when special testing is being conducted.

COX COMMUNICATIONS, Cleveland, OH (2001–2009)
Operator Mechanic
Responsibilities included daily inspection of all mechanical, electrical, and electronic equipment; chemical analysis of all water systems; preventative maintenance and repairs on plant equipment; and writing work orders for discrepancies.

LINCOLN ELECTRIC, Cleveland, OH (2000–2001)
Mechanical Design Manufacturing Engineer
Responsibilities included designing the in-house manufacturing equipment. Conceptualized equipment and tested the feasibility of the designs. Applied detailed analysis, design, fabrication, installation, debugging techniques, validation, and documentation. Used mechanical engineering theory and practice toward the design of all equipment.

Submitted by Brenda Thompson

In this example of a combination-format resume, skills are detailed up front and chronological work experience is listed later.

UNITED STATES NAVY, Norfolk, VA (1997–2000)
Nuclear Electronics Technician Second Class
Completed more than 4,000 hours of reactor operating time and more than 7,000 hours of logged maintenance and troubleshooting of electronic and microprocessor-based equipment. Duties included repair and maintenance technician, departmental technical librarian, and repair section supervisor of the ship's calibration lab.

EDUCATION

Cleveland State University, Cleveland, OH (2000–2006)
Major: Electrical Engineering
Credits: 64 college semester credits with an overall GPA of 3.68.

NAVY NUCLEAR POWER SCHOOL, Charleston, NC (1996–1997)
- Training consisted of a 24-week course in science and technology designed to provide theoretical background knowledge of nuclear power. It is presumed each officer has successfully completed at least one year of college-level physics and calculus, including integral calculus.

NAVY ELECTRONICS TECHNICIAN SCHOOL, Orlando, FL (1995–1996)
Certification: Electronics Technician
- A seven-month course concentrating on electricity and electronics, communications systems, digital logic, microprocessor-based equipment, and radar.
- Training consisted of the study of how to interpret schematic diagrams and use appropriate test equipment as well as hands-on experience on how to isolate and correct faults in both military and civilian electronic equipment.

(216) 333-1234   djacobs01@yahoo.com

Paula Redford

1112 W. 73rd St., New York, NY 10023
212-555-5555
predford@xyz.com

SUMMARY

ESL/TOEFL Instructor with proven ability to teach adults of all levels of proficiency with varied educational and business backgrounds. Experience includes teaching conversational and written English. Knowledge of multiple cultures through travel and continuing contacts with people throughout Europe, Asia, South America, and Africa.

EXPERIENCE

ESL Instructor—New York Language Institute, New York, NY   1997–Present

- Teach ESL to private students and business executives; customize lessons according to occupation and level of English proficiency.
- Prepare students for the TOEFL exam.

ESL Instructor—Rutgers University   1997
Language Institute for English (L.I.F.E.) summer program at
The Juilliard School at Lincoln Center, New York, NY

- Taught specialized program for international musicians to improve English proficiency.

ESL and TOEFL Instructor—Pace University, New York, NY   1994–1996

- Taught ESL classes, from beginner to advanced levels, to American immigrants.

Previous experience includes positions as medical administrator at hospitals and for research programs, also tour guide and museum docent.

EDUCATION

B.A., *magna cum laude,* Columbia University, New York, NY

Graduate Studies:
New York University, teaching methodology and applied linguistics
New School for Social Research, language learning and teaching

License:
New York State Teacher's License #1234

Submitted by Wendy Gelberg

This resume disguises a candidate's age. Only the most recent and relevant jobs are included and graduation date is omitted. Would you guess that this candidate is 81 years old?

Sam R. Wilson

3720 Broadview Terrace
Cedarville, OH 45314

s6496889@yahoo.com

(937) 641-0018 (Home)
(937) 649-6889 (Cell)

SALES & MANAGEMENT

Food Industry

FOCUS

Management professional with a distinguished 16-year career that will benefit gross margin improvement, comparable store sales, teamwork productivity, and effective merchandising.

SALES & MANAGING EXPERIENCE

Operations Manager—*Pete's Meat Market,* Cedarville, OH   2010–Present

- Directed training, merchandising, and department sets.
- Category management of the entire market prior to opening.
- Directly responsible for $290K in sales the first 2 months of business.
- Weekly sales increases the first 10 weeks of 2011.
- Established and cultivated positive vendor relations.

Store Manager—*Stop 'n' Go Market,* Cedarville, OH   2004–2010

- Increased wine sales 150% from 2005–2010.
- Increased net profits by 3% per annum beginning in 2006.
- Sales growth of 15% from 2007–2010.

Store Director—*Jerry's Food Markets,* Cedarville, OH   2003–2004

- Reduced backroom inventory $100K in first quarter of 2003.
- Consistently exceeded company sales and gross profit objectives.
- Effectively supervised 8 department managers and over 100 employees.
- Reduced labor costs from 8.1% to 6.1% to add to bottom-line profits.

Meat Department Manager—*Jerry's Food Markets,* Cedarville, OH   1995–2002

- Exceeded gross profit and labor objectives consistently.
- Highest-volume meat department with 10% sales increases annually.
- Acted as interim store manager in absence of market directors.

EDUCATION

- **Spartan Foods Training Courses 1996–2004:** "Wings of the Future," "Sanitation," "Positive Discipline," "Effective Time Management," "Leadership," "Department Sales Growth," and "Merchandising"
- **Zig Zigler "See You At the Top" Motivational Seminar,** 2002—graduated first in class

Submitted by Terri Ferrara

This resume's focus statement quickly summarizes the candidate's experience and tells how a company can benefit from hiring him. Job titles are easy to read due to use of boldfacing, indents, and white space.

Kristina R. Hill

1228 Cedar Ridge Avenue ♦ White Marsh, MD 21162
(301) 555-5019 – Home ♦ (240) 555-2735 – Cell ♦ krh@msn.com

Job Target **Value** **Offered**	**Receptionist ♦ Customer Service ♦ Office Support**

- Personable and friendly; good conversationalist, with excellent face-to-face and telephone communication skills.
- Active listener who demonstrates an innate ability to ask the right questions at the right time.
- Task oriented with an ability to balance strong interpersonal skills with need for efficiency.
- Down-to-earth and practical; place high value on following procedures.
- Patient, persistent, and diplomatic while providing explanations.
- Extremely attentive to detail and producing high-quality work.
- Methodical about gathering information and data to present logical and systematic approaches to completing tasks.
- Artistic and creative; keen sense of style, balance, and use of color.
- Computer literate with self-taught skills in Windows, Internet, e-mail, basic word processing, and keyboarding.

Employment History

Gained cross-functional office and customer service experience through various short-term positions while raising family and maintaining household.

- Supported business office operations for **Rich Lighting.** Managed incoming calls, assisted customers in selecting lighting fixtures, operated cash register, verified credit purchases, and tracked product inventory.
- Demonstrated and sold new and used cars for **Bowman Chevrolet.** Provided customers with information about vehicle features and benefits; completed extensive paperwork; set up and maintained account filing system; prospected for new business by phone and mail solicitation.
- Took over store management for Hagerstown branch of **Carpet Town,** including opening and closing responsibilities; customer service and sales; securing customer financing and calculating interest rates; office filing; and scheduling of installation projects.
- Answered phones, set up filing system, and helped organize office for a newly established restaurant/pub.
- Created and sold hand-drawn greeting cards. Designed and distributed monthly newsletter for Williamsport Amvets Post. Designed covers for high school graduation and baccalaureate pamphlets.

Education

Graduate, **Wye Mills High School,** Wye Mills, MD

Vocational Studies, **Commercial Art,** Career Studies Center, Wye Mills, MD

Submitted by Norine Dagliano

This resume mentions the candidate's ability to learn computer applications on her own. It also explains the time she was out of the workforce to raise children.

LISA J. CARTER

185 Spring Lane ◆ Plantsville, CT 06479-1018 ◆ 860-555-2222 ◆ lisajcarter@hotmail.com

ADMINISTRATIVE PROFESSIONAL

PROFILE

Detail-oriented, accurate, and observant. Well-organized and proficient at multitasking. Excellent customer service aptitude. Outstanding interpersonal and communication skills. Quick learner who can rapidly retain information. Team player who easily establishes rapport and trust. Bilingual—English and Spanish. Computer skills include Microsoft Word, Excel, PowerPoint, and Outlook. Part-time student available for first and second shift.

CORE SKILLS

- Administrative Support
- Procedure Development
- Appointment Scheduling
- Correspondence
- Research & Analysis
- Event Coordination
- Customer Service
- Record Keeping
- Reception

EMPLOYMENT HISTORY

CONNECTICUT SAVINGS BANK   Hartford, CT   9/07 to Present
Administrative Assistant—Mortgage Department

- Process and prepare correspondence and documents for department director.
- Organize new client files. Maintain and update existing files and records.
- Respond to clients' in-person and phone inquires. Provide rate information.
- Conduct ongoing research on competitor products and services.
- Orchestrate administrative functions, including appointment scheduling, filing, and faxing.
- Arranged office promotional events, including Mortgage Education Night.
- *Researched and wrote 27-page office procedure manual adopted for use by 10 branches.*

THE COFFEE STAND   Waterbury, CT   5/95 to 9/07
Shift Supervisor/Sales Associate

- Oversaw activities, efforts, and training of 12 sales associates.
- Coordinated assignments and work schedules. Addressed and corrected shift problems.
- Assisted with processing customer orders, cleaning, and stocking.
- Balanced cash registers and processed bank deposits.
- *Received 2006 Employee of the Year Award in recognition of 55% sales increase.*

EDUCATION

SOUTHERN CONNECTICUT STATE UNIVERSITY, New Haven, CT
Completing Master of Science (Part Time) ◆ Anticipated Date of Graduation—May 2012 (GPA 3.9/4.0)

UNIVERSITY OF CONNECTICUT, Storrs, CT
May 2009 ~ **B.A. in History** (GPA 3.2/4.0)

Submitted by Ross Primack

The top third of Lisa's resume provides critical information about the hard and soft skills she offers a prospective employer. Her employment history is presented in an easy-to-follow format. Achievements in both positions are quantified and emphasized in boldface italics.

Dan T. Harper

265 Charlotte Street, Asheville, NC 28801
(828) 254-7893 *Home*, (828) 230-1421 *Cell*

Heavy Equipment Operator

"I could pick an egg up off the ground and not break it."

PROFILE

DEPENDABLE, PATIENT HARD-WORKER with more than 30 years of experience in aggregate business operating **Drag Line** (9 years), **988 Loader** (7 years), **Hydraulic Shovel** (5 years), **Crane** (3 years), **Bulldozer** (3 years), **Trackhoe** (3 years), **Off-Road Truck** (2 years), and **Jaw Crusher** (1 year). Experience on computerized equipment.

SUMMARY OF STRENGTHS

- At work 30 minutes early *always*.
- Willing to stay as long as it takes to get the job done.
- *Never* miss work.
- Willing to do whatever I'm asked.
- Machine-friendly—easy on equipment; keep it well maintained and clean. Often put on older equipment because I don't tear it up.
- Excellent record for safety of life and equipment.
- Friendly and even-tempered; get along very well with co-workers.
- Keep production as high as possible.
- Know the relationship to company bottom line.

WORK HISTORY

BOONE GRAVEL—Asheville, NC   1980–Present
Portable plant, a subsidiary of RA Julius Industries, Mooreville, NC

- Use crane to tear down rock crusher, conveyor belts, bends, loaders, and backhoes; transport plant to where it is needed and put it back up, as often as three times a year.
- Have worked on large and small projects all over North Carolina in all kinds of weather, including 7 degrees below zero.
- Projects include road and interstate highway construction (including pulling river stone out of rivers, crushing, and transporting to highway site), opening up new quarries (clearing land, removing overburden), and commercial construction.
- Train operators on trackhoe, loader, and off-road truck on safety and operation.

EDUCATION

City High School, Owensville, NC
High School Diploma, 1980

ADDITIONAL TRAINING

Hundreds of hours of training: North Carolina Safety courses (1-day annual refresher training).

Submitted by Dayna Feist

The quote from the candidate himself speaks to his high skill level. The summary shows exactly how he contributes to company profits. Loyal and loved by his company, Dan has worked for the same company his entire career.

KEN SANBORN

97 Moose Trail Path ▪ P.O. Box 1020 ▪ Soldotna, AK 99660
H: (907) 260-5987 ▪ C: (907) 631-2701 ▪ sanbornhunts@msn.com

PROFILE

Industrious and dependable professional with 2 years of oil field experience seeking position as a Driver, Technician, Roustabout, or Expediter. Safety conscious with a QHSE passport. Accustomed to working long hours with demanding schedules in harsh climates and under challenging physical and mental conditions. Solid employment references, strong work ethic, and levelheaded. **Qualifications include**

- ► Valid Class A CDL with HazMat, Tanker, Combo, and Air Brake endorsements and have a perfect driving record. Current N.S.T.C., Hazwoper, and H2S.
- ► 100% drug free, on random drug testing with Worksafe through the U.S. Coast Guard.
- ► No safety incidents during 2 years on the slope; traveled by helicopter daily in one work hitch.
- ► Certified in first aid and CPR with valid endorsements.
- ► Hold a 100 Ton Masters License from the U.S. Coast Guard and can operate other heavy equipment, including bulldozers, loaders, and backhoes.
- ► Knowledgeable about welding and can quickly learn new technical/mechanical skills.

HIGHLIGHTS OF WORK EXPERIENCE

- ▪ Completed 12-week hitches on the slope as both a Straw Boss and Helper in the past 2 years.
- ▪ Run a halibut charter service during the summers, logging 12–16 hours a day, 7 days a week.
- ▪ Currently serve as a Bear Guard and Wildlife Specialist and as a Big Game Guide.
- ▪ Raised and worked on family cattle ranch, performing tasks requiring physical strength and stamina.

EMPLOYMENT HISTORY

MOUNTAIN CAT ENTERPRISES, Helena, MN **Bear Guard and Wildlife Specialist**	2008 to Present
SCHLUTZ OILFIELD SERVICES, Fairbanks, AK **Straw Boss**	2008
ENERGY SERVICES CONTRACTORS, Anchorage, AK **Straw Boss and Helper**	2007
DEEP WATER FISHING, Seward, AK **Charter Operator**	2001 to Present
GREATER SOLDOTNA ALASKAN GUIDE SERVICES, Inc., Soldotna, AK **Big Game Guide**	2000 to Present
HALIBUT RUN CHARTERS, Juneau, AK **Deckhand**	2001
BIG BLUE WATERS CHARTERS, Ninilchik, AK **Deckhand**	2000
D-R-J RANCH, La Paz, CA **Ranch Hand**	1995 to 2000

REFERENCES AVAILABLE UPON REQUEST

Submitted by Jill Grindle

The Professional Profile section clearly notes which jobs the candidate is interested in. Highlights demonstrate his endurance, physical strength, and ability to work under extreme conditions in harsh climates. Because of his diverse work history, often with short-term jobs, a functional format worked best for this candidate.

NOAH S. THOMAS

1029 Joshkate Avenue • Cincinnati, Ohio 45231
(513) 598-9100 • nst@printedpages.com

Profile

Customer-focused manager with diversified experience in the retail/grocery/convenience store and restaurant industries, including stores that sell gasoline. Excellent analytical and problem-solving skills. Dependable and self-reliant; work equally well independently or as part of a team. Quick to learn procedures and assimilate new product knowledge. Core competencies: operations, ordering and inventory control, merchandising, employee scheduling and supervision, payroll, and record keeping. Excellent communication and interpersonal skills; proven ability to teach, lead, and motivate others.

Experience

SUPERSPEED USA, Cincinnati, OH   11/08–Present
General Manager
Total P&L accountability for gas station/convenience store operation (open 24/7). Hired, trained, and supervised 15 employees.

- ▶ Reduced shrinkage 42% by implementing improved internal controls (inventory, receiving) and loss-prevention initiatives.
- ▶ Increased gross margin by more than 2% by focusing on fast-food area.
- ▶ Earned an award for highest increase in fountain beverage sales (out of 100+ stores in the district), 2 consecutive quarters.

FAST FOODS, INC., Cincinnati, OH   9/04–10/08
Unit Manager, Danny's Burgers
Directed the activities of 20 Customer Service Representatives and 2–3 Assistant Managers in all aspects of restaurant operations.

- ▶ Turned around a failing store through a combination of retraining, encouraging teamwork, and controlling costs. Offset losses, producing $7,300 profit the first month and consistent profits ranging from $2,900 to $10,000+ each month thereafter.
- ▶ Improved drive-through speed an average of 32%.
- ▶ Developed computer programs and spreadsheets to schedule employees and track sales by product category and vendor.
- ▶ Recognized as Manager of the Month several times.

Education

CLAREMONT COMMUNITY COLLEGE, Pigeon Forge, TN   2001–2004
Completed classes in data processing, accounting, marketing, and management.

Computer Skills

Proficient with MS Office (Word, Excel, Access), FoodSys, various Internet search engines, and e-mail programs.

Submitted by Michelle Mastruserio Reitz

Job duties are kept in paragraph form while accomplishments are bulleted for emphasis. The resume downplays the candidate's lack of a college degree.

OBJECTIVE

A management position in operations or logistics in the retail industry.

SUMMARY OF QUALIFICATIONS

Twenty-four years of experience in leadership, command, and senior staff positions in medium and large complex organizations. Versatile, dynamic leader and high achiever who communicated positively and effectively with people at all levels of an organization. Demonstrated record of success in creating highly effective teams, logistics management, strategic planning, increasing efficiency, and establishing strong organizational systems.

- **Logistics Distribution**
- **Leadership**
- **Strategic Planning**
- **Organizational Management**
- **Team Building**
- **Training**

ORGANIZATIONAL MANAGEMENT

Supervised all aspects of a large, complex organization of 6,000 personnel. Efficiently executed an annual budget of $42M. Implemented aggressive management controls and cost-reduction initiatives that resulted in the savings of an average of $1M per quarter. Maintained and operated facilities, complex equipment, and vehicles with a total value in excess of $500M. Planned, prepared, and executed organizational oversight for task forces and peace support rotations. Used an active and positive After Action Report process to ensure task forces knew what happened, why it happened, and how they could fix problems.

TRAINING

Created an integrated team training approach to teach, coach, and mentor leaders of medium-sized organizations in all aspects of leadership and training. Prepared them to deploy to contingency locations to assist units as they complete preparations for war or peace. Created an environment where soldiers could focus on training to learn and gain confidence in their war-fighting skills while ensuring soldier and family readiness.

LEADERSHIP

Led and commanded small, medium, and large organizations of up to 6,000 personnel. Commanded a large multiservice organizational team of 6,000 personnel in Iraq and a medium organization of 1,000 in Afghanistan. Coordinated the efforts and activities of army units, international humanitarian organizations, and nongovernmental agencies. Cited by General Officers for "always leading my soldiers from the front and never asking them to do anything I would not do myself" and "moving my command without regard for personal danger to ensure it was at the decisive point of the battle, at the right time."

Submitted by James Walker

This retiring army colonel had completed a successful command tour in Iraq and now was assigned to a staff leadership position in anticipation of his retirement. His skills are emphasized in a functional format.

(continued)

(continued)

LOGISTICS DISTRIBUTION AND MANAGEMENT

Created and maintained a complex logistics distribution network with thousands of lines of supply both in the United States and Iraq. Aggressive leadership and planning ensured on-time delivery and minimal lag time. Implemented highly effective systematic maintenance procedures and user responsibilities in the supply warehouse, resulting in increased readiness rates and better asset visibility.

STRATEGIC PLANNING

Helped develop and execute the Fort Riley strategic training and logistics plans. Negotiated with numerous Iraqi, U.S. governmental officials, and other foreign nationals in planning and implementing a regional strategy for reconstruction. Responsible for administering $23.5 million in Iraqi reconstruction money. Effectively managed combat and civil affairs operations to support local governance initiatives as well as training for emerging Iraqi Security Forces.

TEAM BUILDING

Planned, funded, and constructed a series of bases in Iraq exceeding $20M. Teamed with the Corps of Engineers, international contractors, and organizational units to complete the projects efficiently and effectively. Fostered a sense of cooperation and trust with rotational units that fed on my infectious enthusiasm and passion for learning how to lead, fight, and win. Created a command climate that was professional, healthy, stimulating, and extremely supportive for young officers and junior leaders.

EMPLOYMENT HISTORY

- Director for Operations and Logistics, U.S. Army, Fort Riley, KS, November 2009–Present
- Commander, U.S. Army, Iraq and Fort Riley, KS, June 2008–October 2009
- Commander, U.S. Army, Fort Carson, CO, June 2007–May 2008
- Training Director, U.S. Army, Heidelberg, Germany, June 2005–June 2007
- Commander, U.S. Army, Afghanistan and Fort Bragg, NC, May 2003–May 2005

EDUCATION

- Graduate, Military Strategic Studies, 1 year, U.S. Army War College, Carlisle, PA
- Master of Science, Strategy, U.S. Army War College, Carlisle Barracks, PA
- Master of Arts, History, Temple University, Philadelphia, PA
- Bachelor of Science, Engineering, United States Military Academy, West Point, NY

DOLORES SMITH

2092 Recreation Drive • Powell, Ohio 43065
Home: 614-890-4499 • Cell: 614-276-4544
E-mail: dolores@worthingtonma.com

COSMETIC ARTISTRY • COSMETIC SUPPLY SALES • PROFIT CENTER MANAGEMENT

Leading-Edge Cosmetology Techniques/Methods • Esthetic • Spa Profit Protocols

Customer-oriented cosmetology professional with valuable blend of business ownership and management experience combined with noticeable talent in esthetic skin care leading to enhanced appearance and well-being of customers; utilizing 25-year history as licensed **Cosmetologist, Manager, and Instructor** to propel all facets of client care, organizational management, and strategic planning agendas. Extremely well organized, dedicated, and resourceful with ability to guide operations and associates to **technique improvements, maximized productivity, and bottom-line increases.**

AREAS OF STRENGTH

- Relationship Building • Customer Service •
- Time Management • Creative/Strategic Selling •
- Follow-Up • Merchandising/Promotion •
- Relationship Management •
- Product Introduction • Inventory Management •
- Expense Control • Vendor Negotiations •
- Client Needs Analysis •

EDUCATION

FINER ACADEMY OF COSMETOLOGY ... Finer, Ohio
• Cosmetology • Manager • Instructor •
Licenses

FINER ACADEMY OF HAIR DESIGN ... Finer, Ohio
Graduate in Hair Design

SEMINARS & SPECIALIZED TRAINING

Continuing Education Units
(to meet requirements of 8 credits annually)

Certificate of Achievement for Advanced Basic
Esthetics and Spa Therapies, August 2009

Several seminars held by various cosmetics
associations

ADDITIONAL BACKGROUND

The Hair Artists ... Dublin, Ohio
Manager of Licensed Cosmetologists
(1998–2001)

Jean Benet Salon ... Worthington, Ohio
Licensed Cosmetologist
(1995–1998)

PROFESSIONAL EXPERIENCE

STUDIO D@RENÉ.....DUBLIN, Ohio (May 2001 to October 2010)
Full-service and independent customized hair, nails, and tanning boutique positioned in strip-mall (suburban locale) setting; operations staffed by 5 employees, contractors, and technicians.

Owner/General Manager
Directed total operation while simultaneously contributing as cosmetologist in one of four-station salon; as single owner of small business, administered profit and loss, undertook all facets of decision-making, strategically guided salon operations and productivity, and assumed complete responsibility for revenue performance.

Management responsibilities included cosmetic and accessories sales, customer service, client management, accounting, finance, recruiting/hiring/training/scheduling, compliance, business/operations legal requisites, retail merchandising, advertising, inventory procurement/control, vendor relationships, contract negotiations, booth rental contracts, and leases to licensed cosmetologists and nail technicians.

→ **Successfully conceived and launched full scale of operations** and guided business to strong reputation for quality output of product and services; consistently met challenges of market conditions and business atmosphere to persevere throughout 8 years of ownership.

→ **Maintained operating costs at lowest possible point by reducing inventory and labor hours during seasonal periods;** also negotiated with vendors to secure better pricing for goods and services.

→ **Facilitated revenue increase by bringing in cosmetic line to enhance product offering to clients.**

→ **Recognized revenue opportunity** and spearheaded remodel of existing tanning space to provide for salon.

→ **Expanded market visibility by becoming member of Powell Chamber of Commerce.**

→ **Modified policies and procedures to ensure employee compliance with changing licensing regulations.**

→ **Worked in concert with American Cancer Society to provide styling services to cancer patients** with aims at improving appearance, outlook, confidence, and self-esteem.

Submitted by Jeremy Worthington

The candidate's name and expertise stand out in this bold presentation. The two column-format enables her to pack lots of information on one page.

6345 Highland Boulevard
Minneapolis, Minnesota

June 28, XXXX

Mr. James A. Blackwell
Vice President, Engineering
Acme Revolving Door Company
New Brunswick, Pennsylvania 21990

Dear Mr. Blackwell:

I graduated from the University of Minnesota this spring with a 3.66 grade average and a Bachelor of Science Degree in Mechanical Engineering.

Your company has been highly recommended to me by my uncle, John Blair, the Pennsylvania District Governor for Rotary, International. He has appreciated your friendship and business relationship over the years and has advised me to forward my resume. My own reading in business publications has kept me aware of the new products that Acme has marketed. Also, I recently visited your excellent Web site and was impressed with the variety of materials you produce.

My objective is to design mechanical parts for a privately owned company that enjoys an excellent reputation and that conducts business internationally.

I hope that I may take the liberty of calling your office to see if we might meet to discuss possible opportunities with Acme. I plan to be in Pennsylvania toward the end of next month, and this might provide a convenient time to meet, if your schedule permits.

Sincerely,

Patricia Dugan
(612) 555-3445

This letter, which was not written for a particular job opening, mentions a mutual friend to help introduce the candidate and establish a relationship.

July 10, XXXX

Mr. Paul Resley
Operations Manager
Rollem Trucking Co.
1-70 Freeway Drive
Kansas City, Missouri 78401

Mr. Resley:

I obtained your name from the membership directory of the Affiliated Trucking Association. I have been a member for over 10 years, and I am very active in the Southeast Region. The reason I am writing is to ask for your help. The firm I had been employed with has been bought by a larger corporation. The operations here have been disbanded, leaving me unemployed.

While I like where I live, I know that finding a position at the level of responsibility I seek may require a move. As a center of the transportation business, your city is one I have targeted for special attention. A copy of my resume is enclosed for your use. I'd like you to review it and consider where a person with my background would get a good reception in Kansas City. Perhaps you could think of a specific person for me to contact?

I have specialized in fast-growing organizations or ones that have experienced rapid change. My particular strength is in bringing things under control, then increasing profits. While my resume does not state this, I have excellent references from my former employer and would have stayed if a similar position existed at its new location.

As a member of the association, I hoped that you would provide some special attention to my request for assistance. I plan on coming to Kansas City on a job-hunting trip within the next six weeks. Prior to my trip I will call you for advice on who I might contact for interviews. Even if they have no jobs open for me now, perhaps they will know of someone else who does.

My enclosed resume lists my phone number and other contact information should you want to reach me before I call you. Thanks in advance for your help on this.

Sincerely,

John B. Goode
Treasurer, Southeast Region
Affiliated Trucking Association

John B. Goode

---

312 Smokie Way   Nashville, Tennessee 31201

This letter written to accompany an unsolicited resume explains why the candidate is leaving his old job and includes positive information about his references and skills that would not normally be found in a resume. John asks for an interview even though there might not be any jobs open now, and also asks for names of others to contact.

1768 South Carrollton Street
Nashville, Tennessee 96050
May 26, XXXX

Ms. Karen Miller
Office Manager
Lendon, Lendon, and Sears
Suite 101, Landmark Building
Summit, New Jersey 11736

Dear Ms. Miller:

Enclosed is a copy of my resume that describes my work experience as a legal assistant. I hope this information will be helpful as background for our interview next Monday at 4 p.m.

I appreciate your taking time to describe your requirements so fully. This sounds like a position that could develop into a satisfying career. And my training in accounting — along with experience using a variety of computer programs — seems to match your needs.

Lendon, Lendon, and Sears is a highly respected name in New Jersey. I am excited about this opportunity and I look forward to meeting with you.

Sincerely,

Richard Wittenberg

This letter was sent to a hiring manager before a scheduled interview. It introduces the resume, shows how the candidate fits the job, and conveys enthusiasm ahead of the interview.

ALBAROSA BARTON
12603 SOUTH 33rd STREET
OMAHA, NEBRASKA 68123
PHONE (402) 292-9052
FAX (402) 393-0099
EMAIL ALBAROSA@OFCORPS.COM

March 30, XXXX

YALE BUSINESS SERVICES
Alexander Bell, Director of Human Resources
1005 Denver Street, Suite 1
Bellevue, Nebraska 68005-4145

Dear Mr. Bell:

I am enclosing a copy of my resume for your consideration and would like to call your attention to the skills and achievements in my background that are most relevant.

I am an achiever, with four years of experience as a highly successful administrator. I've always set high standards and consistently achieved my goals. I've served in the United States Air Force since February 1998 as an Administrative Specialist/ Assistant. I acquired my training through the excellent programs the Air Force provides. I am highly motivated and would be a dynamic administrator for whatever company I represent.

I am confident in my administrative abilities and have already proven myself in the areas of office administration and customer relations.

I look forward to hearing from you soon and having the opportunity to discuss your needs and plans.

Cordially,

ALBAROSA BARTON

This is a cover letter written by an air force administrator transitioning to a civilian career.

4550 Parrier Street
Espinosa, California 44478

August 11, XXXX

Mr. Craig Schmidt
District Manager
Desert Chicken Shops
Post Office Box 6230
Los Angeles, California 98865

Dear Mr. Schmidt:

My resume (enclosed) outlines my four years of successful experience as a fast food manager
with a nationwide network of restaurants. I graduated from a Restaurant Management curriculum
at Harman University with a 3.75 GPA in 1998.

I have been impressed with the rapid growth and exceptional quality of product and service for
which Desert Chicken has become well known. This is the kind of organization I hope to work
for now.

My experience includes positions as cook, night manager, assistant manager, and manager for
my current employer.

I will call your office in a few days to see if we might schedule a convenient time to meet and
discuss some areas of mutual interest.

Thanks very much for your consideration.

Sincerely,

Douglas Parker

Enclosure

This cover letter was written to a company with no advertised openings. It
closes with a promise to contact the hiring manager in hopes of setting up a
meeting, rather than a more passive closing.